CORE TEXTS AND CULTURE

Working Together in Liberal Education

Selected Papers from the Tenth Annual Conference
of the Association for Core Texts and Courses
Dallas, Texas
April 15–18, 2004

Edited by
Ronald J. Weber
J. Scott Lee
Mary Buzan
Anne Marie Flanagan
Douglas Hadley
Cynthia Rutz
Thomas Sorger

University Press of America,® Inc.
Lanham · Boulder · New York · Toronto · Plymouth, UK

Copyright © 2010 by
University Press of America,® Inc.
4501 Forbes Boulevard
Suite 200
Lanham, Maryland 20706
UPA Acquisitions Department (301) 459-3366

Estover Road
Plymouth PL6 7PY
United Kingdom

All rights reserved
Printed in the United States of America
British Library Cataloging in Publication Information Available

Library of Congress Control Number: 2009938120
ISBN: 978-0-7618-4936-0 (paperback : alk. paper)
eISBN: 978-0-7618-4937-7

™ The paper used in this publication meets the minimum
requirements of American National Standard for Information
Sciences—Permanence of Paper for Printed Library Materials,
ANSI Z39.48-1992

Table of Contents

Introduction   vii

Community: History and Forms

Humanizing the Technological Vision:
Core Learning and the Relation of the Sciences and Humanities
Phillip R. Sloan   3

Plato's *Crito* and the Development of Community
David Shiner   17

Augustine's Intellectual Conversion
Richard M. Liddy   25

Views of Community

Beowulf: The Other Epic
Christine Cornell   33

Montesquieu and the Problematic Character
of Modern Citizenship
Matthew Davis 39

Kleos and Kitsch:
Postcard Patriotism in Derek Walcott's *Omeros*
Joel Garza 45

Lyric and the Skill of Life
Eileen Gregory 53

Achieving (Comm) Unity in Difference
Through the Core Text
D.W. Hadley 61

Literary Experiences of Community

The Music of Democracy: Core Values in Core Texts
Paul Woodruff 71

Nature and Tyranny in Aristophanes' *Birds*:
The Real Meal Deal
Anne Leavitt 87

Lyric Breath: Taking Seriously the Trope of Immortality
in Shakespeare's *Sonnets*
Scott F. Crider 97

Whose Underground?: Notes on Locating Dostoyevsky
Margaret Heller 103

Community: New Perspectives

Art, Integrating Disciplines, and Liberal Education:
Imagining the Possible with Botticelli
J. Scott Lee 113

Culture and Patriarchy:
The Egalitarian Vision of Woolf's *Three Guineas*
James Woelfel   123

Spoken from the Heart:
Apprehending the Passion of Harriet Beecher Stowe
Elizabeth Dell   129

Constructing and Deconstructing the Gospel of John
Lillian I. Larsen   135

Building Communities: Possibilities and Problems

The "Mythical Method" as a Means to Community
in Eliot's *Murder in the Cathedral*
Celia S. Clay   143

Captain Vere, Liberal Learning, and Leadership
Daniel G. Lang   149

"Shall I Ever Attain My Heart's Desire?"
or How a Flexible Approach to Core Texts
is Building Layers of Community at Hanover College
Jeffrey Brautigam   155

Educating for Justice:
Service Learning and Plato's *Republic*
Jane Kelley Rodeheffer   161

Bridging the Gaps Between the Humanities and Sciences

Natural Philosophy as a Liberal Art
J.H. Beall — 169

Euclid as Propadeutic
Patricia Cook — 183

Stealing the Power and Bridging the Gap:
Ellison's *Invisible Man* as Core Text
Page Laws — 189

Connecting Principles in Adam Smith's
History of Astronomy
Charles Sullivan — 195

Darwin Redux: Great Texts
and the Natural Sciences Revisited
Keith Francis — 203

Introduction

Throughout its existence, in multiple forums, the Association for Core Texts and Courses (ACTC) has asserted its commitment to the need for humans to come together to speak about the scientific, the political, and the artistic in order to live together in an enlightened fashion. In 2004, ACTC's Tenth Annual Conference convened to re-affirm and re-examine the value of serious reading and serious discussion focused through core texts. The conference challenged participants to articulate the various ways by which core text education in the liberal arts constructs and supports different expressions of community on college campuses around the world. In turn, presenters confronted a tension facing liberal core text education by asking whether it is better to contemplate the arts simply as expressions of cultures and traditions or to cultivate them, taking the risk that what is valued in artistic expressions might be changed by the inventions of teachers and the students they encourage. The essays collected here reflect the responses of the diverse group of ACTC's members, all of whom support the idea of liberal core text education with the self-conscious awareness of the challenges facing liberal education in the modern academy.

Each section of this volume represents a true dialog on liberal education. Juxtaposed with one another, contributors explore the internal challenges within the union of core text supporters and the external opposition from advocates of the practical and the relevant. On the one hand, as the papers show, there is a passion in ACTC to preserve and perpetuate expressions of truth and beauty. It stems from the commitment to core texts as works of such major cultural significance that were they not made available to students, those students would lose something vital in their efforts to become liberally educated. On the other hand, this set of academic authors realizes that passion without control can foster over-specialization and compromise ACTC's interdisciplinary approach, which seeks to blend society's call for practical learning with education in the arts and humanities. Remarkably, while this collection reflects many different approaches to liberal education from a variety of disciplines, in the end the areas of agreement are significant.

Internally and externally one of the most frequently cited arguments against liberal core text education is that the traditions of core texts are in direct conflict with the values and goals of the present. It is true that contemporary voices can and do articulate essential truths in more timely settings. However, as these discussions show, to privilege more contemporary voices to the exclusion of past ideas is to ignore the continuity of human existence. Such privileging denies the origins of current wisdom and overlooks the pitfalls that lead to extremes that isolate and divide the community of people and ideas. In the end, it is the ability of core text study to provide continuity, which unifies the disparate contributors to this collection, as they dialog about both the pros and cons of the process of core text education. The consensus of their work is that core text education is powerful because:

1. it is based upon sound learning principles which have retained their value over time;
2. it spans diverse and comprehensive racial, geographical and subject areas, encompassing a true breadth of knowledge.
3. it fosters community;
4. it utilizes the past to realize the present and build for the future;
5. its common elements bridge the gaps between seemingly diverse disciplines such as the humanities and science; and,
6. by fostering works with well-developed styles and complex vocabularies, it promotes advanced literacy and expression.

Twenty-two papers and three plenary addresses make up this volume. The first section, "Community: History and Focus," begins with the address of ACTC's president, Phillip R. Sloan. His address outlines the history of community building through liberal core text education and discusses two of the most influential texts in the canon, Plato's *Crito* and St. Augustine's *Confessions*. Together, these texts question the basic, elemental tension within society between concern for the individual and the good of the community. Plato approached these ethical concerns as an exercise in common sense. Augustine, basing himself in Platonic essentials, created the ultimate self-help manual. In the variety and complexity of their language, the depth of their thought, their realism and their ethics they encapsulate the universality of the human need for community.

Plato and Augustine are essential to understanding historical communities because they demonstrate how the elements of culture and history form both the possibilities and the problems of any age. In the second section, "Views of Community" takes up the theme across time and genre by examining five different authors who have realized the meaning and importance of community in human experience. At a critical juncture in history, as Christians struggled to understand and evaluate the importance of their pre-Christian heritage, the adventures of Beowulf offered perspective on the impermanence of human creations. In contrast, while the Beowulf poet had wrestled with the place of courage, generosity, honor and loyalty in the community, in his time Montesquieu lamented their dissemblance in the modern commercial republic where the operations of the adversarial nature of business and governance generate indifference and enmity among fellow citizens. Derek Walcott's *Omeros* is seen for vibrantly denouncing the "postcard" nature of such a world. And in their times Emily Dickinson and Sigmund Freud are examples of how to fight off the isolation and depersonalization that the world imposes, and realize the "skill of life" that comes from the knowledge generated by the acute apprehension resulting from loss.

"Literary Expressions of Community"—the third section—continues the discussion, elaborating the five principles of the ideal Greek democratic community: harmony, equality, freedom, reverence, and justice, which in theory are wonderful to hear. However, Aristophanes, with his own brand of biting satire reminds us in the true spirit of open discussion and inquiry that Athenian society too often missed the standards it so smugly extolled. There is no doubt that Aristophanes had little respect for the Athenian capacity for truthful self-examination. Athenian hubris lacked respect for others that, the lyric poetry of Shakespeare's sonnets reminds us, lies at the base of genuine self-realization. Sympathy for the emotions of others bridges the gaps between individuals, setting the stage for true appreciation of differences and unity of action. Dostoyevsky is thus a fitting conclusion to this dialogue as he plumbs the differences between Russian culture and western traditions trying to reconcile this clash of similar but different civilizations.

The stage, thus, has been set for the fourth section, "Community: New Perspectives," which does not look away from tradition but analyzes how tradition can be used to look in directions perhaps not originally intended but ever so important as knowledge evolves. The genius of all artists is their sensitivity to the nuances of life. They are the mentors of understanding in every age. While great authors, poets, artists, architects, and scientists provide windows into the past, each age also requires its own interpreters, those special individuals who focus life. For example, a look at Sandro Botticelli's *Adoration of the Magi* from the perspective of Joshua Reynolds illustrates how visual language clarifies every age. Ancient kings dressed in contemporary garb place the present into history to "enunciate a current reality and, perhaps, a future to be imagined." Virginia Woolf, however, reminds us that tradition is not inherently useful; it must be interpreted for use. Woolf was one of those great interpreters who called for a revolution of cultural definitions and the divisions among people. She stands in sharp contrast to Harriet Beecher Stowe, an author often ridiculed for her racial insensitivity. And yet, when seen as the epiphany of a devout nineteenth-century woman, Stowe's work offers significant insight into the life of a woman who grew to realize the reality of slavery's horrors. So, regardless of how it is used in currently accepted political speech, *Uncle Tom's Cabin* truly defined an age not only in how it reacted to slavery but also in how it reflected the evolving consciousness of women. The section concludes with a discussion of the Gospel of John, part of Stowe's tradition, and an element of the memory that has defined life and literature for two millennia.

In the fifth section, "Building Community: Possibilities and Problems" takes up the process of identifying the idiosyncrasies of past experience to build effective new communities. The key is to distill memory in a manner such as Eliot's *Murder in the Cathedral*, which evokes a rich literary tradition using a twelfth-century event. Eliot's prose demonstrates that allusion not only extends into the past, but also looks at things to come. The past is alive. Herman Melville's short novel *Billy Budd* takes the process a step further by warning against the overemphasis of the theoretical and the artificial in liberal core text curriculum. To be effective community builders, the great books must be real, not special or abstract. Bankim Chandra Chatterji's novel *Anandamath* was profoundly real in the midst of the Indian Nationalist Movement of the 1940's. Although set in 1882, in addressing how Imperialism and Post-Colonialism affected identity and community, the novel resonated throughout India. For comparison, the concluding paper of this section documents how a service learning project, completed as students read Plato's *Republic,* helped to lead real students from the shadows of the myth of the cave into the light of real life.

Finally, the sixth section, "Bridging the Gaps Between the Humanities and Sciences," showcases the results of an ACTC Liberal Arts Institute project. Within the Institute humanists and scientists came *together* to build general education, liberal arts curricula that explores the connections among disciplines. Beginning in the "pure sciences" with Isaac Newton and Johannes Kepler, their work discusses how the knowledge of physics is built upon previous knowledge that establishes Natural Philosophy as a true liberal art. Then, a third Institute participant, by using Euclid, one of the world's first true educators, demonstrates that the first principles of learning theory are as basic to science as they are to the humanities. In contrast, Ralph Ellison's *Invisible Man* articulates how science served to dehumanize black people in America. For Ellison, the black man's struggle was a battle of science versus humanities, white power versus black spirituality, with technology as a force to hold down America's people of color. In turn, Adam Smith's *History of Astronomy* endorses the necessity of order in life and ideas, tracing the history of how the body of knowledge as it was organized over time brought sense and feeling to the world. And then the discussion turns to the paragon of humanities-based science, Charles Darwin. In so many aspects of his work, Darwin epitomizes the successful bridging of the gap. His work is flawlessly organized, exquisitely written, historically sound, and illustrated with clear, practical science. There can be no better way to end this volume.

Our thanks to the University of Dallas for their support of the ACTC Liberal Arts Institute in 2004 and their sponsorship of the 2004 conference. We greatly appreciate the generous support for the conference from the Honors Program of Baylor University and the Humanities Program of the University of Texas at El Paso through the endowment of William Mimmack. Special thanks to Carol Huntley Little of the University of Dallas and Linda Tribune at Temple University for their work throughout 2004 on behalf of the conference.

This volume would not be possible without the work of its editors and readers: Mary Buzan, Anne Marie Flannagen, Douglas Hadley, J. Scott Lee, Cynthia Rutz, and Thomas Sorger. Darcy Wudel and Jean-Marie Kauth were tireless in preparing the manuscript. And finally, we wish to thank all of the members of ACTC for their continuing support of core text education: the work of liberal core text education goes on.

Ronald J. Weber
Director, Humanities Program
University of Texas at El Paso

J. Scott Lee
Executive Director
Association for Core Texts and Courses

; **Community: History and Forms**

Humanizing the Technological Vision: Core Learning and the Relation of the Sciences and Humanities

Phillip R. Sloan
University of Notre Dame

It is an honor to address the tenth anniversary meeting of ACTC at a conference devoted to the interface between core text education, culture, and community. In entitling my talk "Humanizing the Technological Vision: Core Learning and the Relation of the Sciences and Humanities," my purpose is to address in a limited way some of the fragmenting forces in the intellectual culture of our universities and colleges surrounding the so-called "two cultures" problem. In my talk last year I made several references to the 1995 Ernest L. Boyer report on Undergraduate education, *Educating Undergraduates in the Research University*, commissioned by the Carnegie Foundation.[1] That report recommended a reform of undergraduate education I characterize primarily as one formed on the model of the education in the natural sciences. The ideal of undergraduate education it advocates emphasizes research, the preparation for graduate specialization, and the encouragement of a dynamic, open-ended inquiry in education. My comments on this were critical, not because I am opposed to the ideals of research or to specialized learning, or even to the forms of education that work effectively in the natural sciences. But when transported to undergraduate education generally, I see them as potentially corrosive, and destructive of humanistic ideals.

I am concerned in this address to continue an exploration of the relationship between the sciences and core liberal education from a different standpoint, and to develop a more historical and theoretical approach to the values of core learning and the challenges of modern science and technology. The aim of my discussion is therefore not to discuss science as a liberal art, but to examine the interface between general liberal education and the sciences as we typically confront them today—big science, grants-funded science, science that seeks domination over nature and even over man. The model of science of which I am thinking is therefore not that supplied by theoretical astronomy or mathematics, but by the collection of empirical inquiries and practices best represented by an area like "molecular biology." This area of research may be very difficult to characterize in terms of some unitary theoretical principles; it is also not easy to delimit these inquiries by reference to a limited set of core texts or specific scientific achievements. We are all aware, nonetheless, that this kind of inquiry has become a powerful force in contemporary science. When these sciences do find expressions in print, the practitioners and theorists often explicate their aims in terms of a Baconian ideal of the application of knowledge for useful ends, rather than a search for contemplative wisdom. Here the designation adopted by some scholars in the area of science and technology studies—"technoscience"—seems a better label for the subject of discussion, denoting an intimate blend of science, applied technology, institutional organization, and economic factors that all seem entangled together in a complicated system of relationships. What can core text education and the humanistic concerns it typically seeks to develop have to do with this kind of science?

My address will examine this question in two sections. The first will offer some reflections on the concept of liberal education, which I think needs to be clarified if we are to understand why a core text approach may be preferable to the kind of undergraduate education which seems to be recommended by the Boyer Report.

In the second half of my address, I shall discuss some of the ways in which core text education can be applied concretely in this dialogue, illustrated by the NEH-ACTC "Bridging the Gap" project in which I have been a participant.

I approach these complex issues both from training and research practice within the natural sciences at one point in my career, and also from my thirty years of teaching within my own core text undergraduate program, the Program of Liberal Studies at Notre Dame, one of the historic great books programs that developed out of the University of Chicago College program. From its beginning in 1950, my own program included science and mathematics in its curriculum as part of the ideal of an education in the classical seven liberal arts—grammar, rhetoric, logic, arithmetic, astronomy, music, and geometry. As a heritage of these historical roots, we continue to give attention in our curriculum to primary texts of literature, philosophy, theology, political theory, and original works in the sciences and mathematics.

But the University in which I reside has changed remarkably around our program in its fifty-four years of existence. My program now finds itself located in the context of a university culture that emphasizes research scholarship, graduate teaching, and disciplinary specialization, and we are surrounded by large science and engineering complexes, with major research groups in chemistry, physics, and molecular biology. Some of you may also exist in contexts that also contain mega-complexes of medical research facilities. How is general liberal education to relate to this kind of scientific enterprise? What contributions can it make to bring our academic cultures together, and even lead to the creation of a larger cultural dialogue that can contribute to the interaction of humane concerns and "technoscience"?

I shall begin by a brief attempt to characterize "liberal" education itself. To do this, I draw upon Professor Bruce Kimball's important history of the idea of liberal education, a work that I feel should be more widely known and studied.[2] In his survey, *Orators and Philosophers: A History of the Idea of Liberal Education*, Professor Kimball offers a broad historical review that ranges from Antiquity to modern American higher education. He frames his narrative around the interaction of two primary traditions defining liberal education in the west. His claim is that these have been persistent traditions, and that in some of their permutations and combinations, they are still interacting in some form today in American higher education. It is not my intent to try to survey the scholarly details in this history, nor the massive scholarship that surrounds the history of the university. Kimball has provided a useful historical narrative, and I will, for these purposes, accept Kimball's classification and move on.

Following a common classification of educational traditions in the humanities,[3] Kimball outlines the *artes liberales* ideal, given shape particularly by Isocrates in an Attic context, but then developed theoretically by the Roman Humanists. In this ideal, the aim of education was the formation of the virtuous citizen-orator, who was to be educated primarily in what were later designated as the arts of the trivium—grammar, rhetoric, logic—skills that were inculcated through the reading and study of exemplary works of the past. The rationale for reading the classics was clear and well justified. Such works provided the student with exemplary models of reasoning, of oratory, of logical argument, and also of moral example. The scientific arts, later designated as the quadrivium—arithmetic, music, geometry, and astronomy—also became part of this education in the liberal arts in late antiquity. On Kimball's analysis, the *artes liberales* tradition, reformed and refracted by the Renaissance humanists and educational reformers of the Reformation, still played an important role in the educational ideals of many institutions in the early American Republic. One might say that it still survives into the present, at least in some dimensions, in the ideals of great books programs like my own.

Kimball traces the second model to the Greek philosophical tradition. This was developed more systematically in the universities of the Middle Ages, following the recovery of the works of classical antiquity in the twelfth century. The classical liberal arts were to be a preparation for training in the higher faculties of law, medicine, and theology, rather than an end in themselves.

On Kimball's analysis, this philosophical model, rather than that drawn from the arts, was the one that was transmuted in the seventeenth and eighteenth centuries through the educational ideals of Bacon, Descartes, Locke and others into a philosophical ideal of education that was open to the new philosophy and the methods of the natural sciences. The educational ideals of Bacon, Descartes, Locke, and of the French Encyclopedists, as extensions of this philosophical ideal, became explicitly devoted to a progressive, practical form of knowledge dedicated to the improvement of human life.[4]

The characteristics Kimball sees as defining this Enlightenment philosophical ideal of liberal education have made it very amenable to scientific reason—mitigated epistemological skepticism, the open-ended search after truth that is assumed to reach no conclusion, the toleration of all points of view, the emphasis on individual judgment. Kimball's survey of numerous college catalogs and program statements on liberal education in the United States from the post-Civil War period supplies substantial evidence that this "enlightenment" conception of liberal education generally replaced that of the *artes liberales*. Particularly when allied with American Pragmatism, it suggested little reason for a study of the tradition or classic works. The goal of liberal education was to "liberate" the mind, free one from prejudice, develop critical thinking, and develop the skills of writing and rhetoric.

My purpose in this thumbnail summary of Kimball's important study is to give us some landmarks around which to position the encounter of the sciences and humanities. If by "liberal education" we mean something allied to the classical *artes liberales* ideal, there are obvious tensions in the interface with science in its modern expressions. It is not even clear what "science," in its Baconian sense, even means when viewed from this tradition. If "liberal education" is meant in the Enlightenment sense, there is considerably more opportunity for dialogue, but the value and rationale for including the study of classic texts as part of this discussion is less evident, and the Boyer ideal of education seems an inevitable result. How then can the inclusion, and even the study of foundational texts of the humanities in the curricula of science courses develop a more fruitful dialogue between natural sciences and the humanistic disciplines?

One way to open this dialogue is to look in more detail at the model of education that is experienced by our students in their science, engineering, and pre-medical courses. Since I went through this form of education myself up to the advanced graduate level, I can speak not only in the abstract, but also autobiographically.

This is a form of education, particularly fashioned by the German and Scottish universities in the nineteenth century, which rendered education through classical texts alien to its goals. The focus is on the efficient transmission of accepted knowledge, and in the German conception, on the ideal of research. The late historian and philosopher of science Thomas Kuhn[5] developed his theory of scientific development and change in large measure out of his own personal experience with this form of education, first as an undergraduate science major, and then as a research graduate student in experimental physics at Harvard. In an important talk I recommend to this audience entitled "The Function of Dogma in Scientific Research," a statement that was delivered at Oxford the year before the appearance of Kuhn's better-known *The Structure of Scientific Revolutions*, Kuhn questioned the popular view of the scientist as "an uncommitted searcher after truth...the explorer of nature—the man who rejects prejudice at the threshold of the laboratory, who collects and examines bare and objective facts...."[6] To the contrary, he characterized the scientist as one educated in a highly dogmatic system, resembling seminary training. As a dogmatic education, foundational questions are not to be explored—what is knowledge? What is nature? What is the warrant for scientific reasoning? Is the calculus true? Such science is also studiously unconcerned with its own history except as an illustration of error or occasionally as a repository for a few heroic exemplar cases, such as Galileo's confrontation with the Church. As developed in more detail in his subsequent *Structure* of 1962, scientific education is depicted by Kuhn as employing an educational model that is focused upon the inculcation of specific current theories, of manipulative skills, and on ways to "get the right answers" through practice on problems and laboratory experiments. The intent of this education is to initiate one into an increasingly narrow inquiry, focused on limited problems defined within the boundaries of accepted theories.

Because the natural sciences and their technological extensions are typically dogmatic about deeper foundations, and avoid such reflections except when forced to do so at times of theoretical crisis, they have been able to develop progressively and maintain precise focus on the solution of limited, and "in-principle" soluble problems. The natural sciences have also been able to develop particularly effective forms of social organization that discipline these inquiries with precision. Modern science is group science. It is funded by competitive grants that must be won from agencies in refereed competitions that define acceptable methods and problem definitions. Individuals now publish cutting edge research in papers, typically with multiple authors in stringently refereed journals, rather than in monographs. The scientific world of a Charles Darwin or John Herschel, individuals who were able to make major scientific developments from their country estates, no longer exists. Even in the nineteenth century this model of science was rapidly disappearing from view, being replaced by the research institute, the funded laboratory, and the graduate university. The science we experience today is continuous with this new organization of science that emerged from the nineteenth century.

In such a model of education, there would seem to be little opportunity or rationale in the sciences for the reading of classic sources and reflection on fundamental principles and deeper metaphysical and epistemological questions. In a famous paper published in *Science* some years ago, it was even suggested, if with subtle irony, that perhaps the science student should be kept away from the history of science. To explore it would only be unsettling.[7]

In the past two decades, exemplified by the growth of the subdiscipline of critical "social studies" of science and technology, the relations between the sciences and humanities have become in some instances openly hostile. In an effort to defang the power of science and technology, and to display the ideological and socially-constructed nature of scientific knowledge, humanistic scholars in the 80s and 90s turned the methods of sociology, history, anthropology, post-modernist literary criticism, and critical philosophical analysis into weapons to be used against the natural sciences. When scientists perceived more clearly these intentions of their humanistic colleagues, the response was in some instances a broadside against the humanities, exemplified by the collaborative work by a marine biologist and mathematician, entitled *Higher Superstition: The Academic Left and its Quarrels With Science*. Their attack was followed by the famous Alan Sokal hoax in 1996, in which a well-known professional physicist published an entirely fictitious theoretical article, complete with 109 footnotes, bearing the impressive title "Transgressing the Boundaries: Towards a Transformative Hermeneutics of Quantum Gravity," in a respected refereed journal of the social studies of science. At the same time he published in another journal an exposé of the obvious scientific incompetence of the reviewers of his quantum gravity article to illustrate the false credentials of those engaged in critical social studies of science.[8]

These kinds of hostile confrontations of the sciences and the humanities do not seem productive. The losers were not the scientists, but the humanists in these encounters. At the same time, these engagements do reflect from the side of the humanities a concern with the growing hegemony of the sciences, with their tendency to subsume all subjects under the domain of scientific rationality, with their failure to reflect on assumptions and foundations, and their tendency to become forms of human domination. The problem, as I see it, is with the terms on which this interface has been conceived. The humanists involved have certainly developed the arts of criticism to a fine degree, but their way of entry into the dialogue lacked the kind of humility before the text and the willingness to give the sciences a properly respectful hearing that I would hope a genuine liberal education would encourage. The Sokal affair also illustrated the danger of outsiders treading into the highly technical world of modern science.

The need for a more productive interfacing of the sciences and humanities is obvious, but how to develop this is not immediately evident. As the Austrian psychotherapist Viktor Frankl wrote in a penetrating essay some years ago, the fault is not with scientific reasoning or even with the effort to find reductive and naturalistic explanations of phenomena, even in such areas as psychology. The problem for the humanities is that scientific "specialists are generalizing" (Frankl 397). By this he means the extension of the claims of science beyond their proper domain to constitute totalizing claims of a metaphysical nature about reality. Any number of leading scientists who have entered the public domain have illustrated this tendency, from Ernst Haeckel and Jacques Loeb at the turn of the nineteenth century, to E. O. Wilson, Stephen Weinberg, Francis Crick, and Richard Dawkins in our own. The comment of Crick, best known for his collaborative work on the structure of DNA with James Watson, but who spent his latter years attempting to give a molecular-biological explanation of consciousness, is illustrative of this tendency to generalize from the sciences to a much broader canvas: "your joys and your sorrows, your memories and your ambitions, your sense of personal identity and free will, are in fact no more than the behavior of a vast assembly of nerve cells and their associated molecules" (Watson, cited in Wertheim, D3). When reading such claims, one wonders if something has not gone very much awry in our education, and in the education in the sciences in particular. It is not just that such claims are inconvenient or threatening; they are also simply paradoxical if drawn out to their logical consequences. If this is the explanation of thinking, what are we to make of Crick's claims themselves?

This tendency for the natural sciences to extend their claims in this way can be traced, I suggest, to the form of education in the sciences itself, to the way in which it inculcates a way of seeing phenomena, and even the world in general, through a limited perspective. In the life sciences, for example, in which I was trained, it means to understand the living being primarily in terms of reductive and analytic categories, and to develop methods to explain the more complex states of life by the functioning of simpler parts. Extension of such insights into a worldview in the way we find manifest in the Crick quote is not surprising.

But with this recognized, the more productive goal that several of us in ACTC have pursued is to seek a model of discussion in which we can fruitfully engage the sciences and humanities in a mutually productive dialogue. I would like to turn to the model of the "Bridging the Gap" seminars as an example of this.

I acknowledge at the outset that there are several ways one might envision opening up a deeper dialogue between the sciences and humanities through pedagogical efforts. One might concentrate on the study of scientific methodology and the philosophy of science in order to create a more critical awareness of the assumptions of the sciences. Another might pursue a curricular model in which humanists and scientists "team teach" courses together, drawing on the different perspectives of each. But the approach of the Bridging the Gap project has taken the route of doing this through the study of primary sources and great experiments. These seminars have also required reading from works from both the traditional humanities and from the works of the sciences.

To approach the discussion in this way is to accomplish two goals. First, it brings to the attention of the participating humanists the difficulty and complexity of inquiry into nature. This has been the particular function of the laboratory experiments. To "see" the phenomena under consideration requires the acquisition of skill through practice that is only accomplished with difficulty.

For the scientists in the group, discussions with experts from the humanities has meant they must encounter scientific texts as literary productions in all their original complexity. While this kind of primary source approach may be familiar to those of us in the humanities, especially those committed to reading the tradition and its sources, this is not familiar territory for the scientists for the reasons alluded to earlier.

When one enters a scientific text from the past, one discovers that what is supposed to be there is in fact not necessarily present, nor present in the way one might expect. One finds in a work like Harvey's treatise on the circulation of the blood, for example, a rhetorical exercise, requiring the skills of argument, and demanding theoretical leaps beyond the evident data. Our participants learned what these data were by doing some actual laboratory dissections along with this reading, which experience enabled them to perceive these leaps more clearly. Similarly, the reader of Mendel's classic paper on plant hybridization is startled to find that Mendel himself seems to find his laws of inheritance ambiguous, and there is no notion of a "gene" in evidence. Reading Darwin's *Origin* reveals that neither is Darwin a "neo-Darwinian" in our sense, nor is one offered much in the way of compelling data by the text itself. Instead one reads a text that is only offered as an abstract of a promised text that was in fact never published, yet for this very reason it was a text that was able to gain a wide readership beyond the circle of scientific experts. What is acquired through the reading of such texts is an appreciation of the interweaving of rhetoric, background assumptions, new ways of seeing phenomena, and empirical experience. To be sure, these literary and rhetorical dimensions are more evident in a text like Galileo's *Dialogues on the Two Chief World Systems* than in a recent scientific paper, but any change of scientific thinking is a matter of persuasion as well as demonstration.

One finds in moving in the other direction that major works of literature may incorporate substantial reflections on the sciences, as we see in Dante's great epic, or in the works of Goethe and Tennyson. We also come to see that the differences between works of literature and science are not as great as one might believe when they are examined from literary perspectives.

Perhaps the most important function of the study of science through its textual sources in our Bridging seminars has been the experience of seeing science, as much as literature or philosophy, as a human activity. It has assumptions that can be examined and critiqued, but the beauty of the sciences is also revealed. Through an education in the great texts of both the sciences and the humane disciplines, our two cultures can see more clearly the claims of both, and the wisdom in both. I would hope those on the humanistic side come to discover the great drive for truth, the willingness to be patient with excruciating detail, the long hours of intense and frustrating research that may be required for even a minor breakthrough in the sciences.

We would hope from this encounter that scientists might be made more willing through the study of sources to reflect on their enterprise, on the difference between methods and metaphysics. The willingness of the sciences to generalize their conclusions into totalizing philosophical programs might in this case be more restrained. We also would hope to generate from this engagement a new level of respect of the two sides of this dialogue for each other's perspectives. Developing a fruitful dialogue between the sciences and humanities, particularly as these exist in the present, will never be an easy task. But a core text approach has demonstrated its viability in creating a new level of dialogue. This neither requires abandoning traditional liberal education to a research ideal, nor the reducing of the sciences to forms that are no longer descriptive of their nature.

The stakes in this discussion are high ones, and the need for fruitful dialogue is pressed upon us by the increasing pressure of technoscience. As a final reflection on this, I will offer a few more general comments. At the roots of the modern scientific age, we find a historic overlap of two figures who offer us some different perspectives on what the new era might bring. To Shakespeare, whose famous lines from the *Tempest* (1623) "O brave new world, that hath such people in't," are uttered within a symbolic disenchantment of the world by the putting away of Prospero's magical arts, it was not clear what lay ahead. To his contemporary Francis Bacon, the "brave new world" was one that would result from applied technology and the domination of nature through empirical methods and the rational organization of knowledge. Bacon's novel conception of science, exemplified by the House of Solomon depicted in the *New Atlantis* of 1627, sought "the knowledge of Causes and secret motions of things; and the enlarging of the bounds of Human Empire, to the effecting of all things possible."

Bacon's view of the new science was always restrained by limits. It was only intended to regain knowledge originally in the possession of mankind. It was not to go beyond this into the pursuit of an unlimited Promethean domination of nature. As Bacon puts this, the new knowledge was neither

> for the pleasure of the mind, or for contention, or for superiority to others, or for profit, or fame, or power, or any of these inferior things, but for the benefit and use of life, and that they perfect and govern it in charity. For it was from lust of power that the angels fell, from lust of knowledge that man fell....

This original Baconian project was, however, altered in the eighteenth century into Baconianism without limits. Science, wedded with technology, was to be the key to a presumably unlimited future, and it was only to be constrained by the interests of mankind. This ideal, codified in the great Encyclopédie of Denis Diderot and Jean D'Alembert that commenced publication in 1751, gave flesh to the Baconian project, demonstrating how the skills of artisans and the rationality of the scientist could be brought together in a grand collaborative enterprise that was finally beginning to realize its goals of the domination of nature through science and technology. Through a complex history I will not attempt to summarize, this Enlightenment project has become our own.

We stand at 250 years distance from these ambitions of the French Enlightenment. We can also see more clearly the ambiguity in this unrestrained Baconianism, the possibility that the drive to a mastery of nature could lead us into Aldous Huxley's rather than Shakespeare's "Brave New World." The sustained reflection on the sciences and the humanities together in our Bridging seminars has been an effort to reflect more deeply on this scientific and technological project, to seek to preserve Miranda's "beauteous mankind" along with our scientific and technological progress.

Notes

1. Available at <http://naples.cc.sunysb.edu/Pres/boyer.nsf>.
2. Bruce R. Kimball, *Orators and Philosophers: A History of the Idea of Liberal Education.*
3. See the similar classification employed by the founder of my own Program, Otto Bird, in his *Cultures in Conflict: An Essay in the Philosophy of the Humanities,* chapter 1.
4. Other commentators, such as Otto Bird and Alasdair MacIntyre, have tended to separate this off as a separate "encyclopedic" ideal rather than attempting to connect it with the pre-existent philosophical tradition of the middle ages. See Bird, *Cultures,* and Alasdair MacIntyre, *Three Rival Versions of Moral Inquiry.*
5. Thomas Kuhn, *The Structure of Scientific Revolutions,* chapter 3-4.
6. Thomas Kuhn, "The Function of Dogma in Scientific Research," *Scientific Change,* chapter 11. This is the proceedings of the Oxford conference of 1961.
7. Stephen Brush, "Should the History of Science be Rated X?"
8. The original article is "Transgressing the Boundaries: Towards a Transformative Hermeneutics of Quantum Gravity," in *Social Text*; his criticism is in *Lingua Franca,* both published in 1996.

Works Cited

Bird, Otto. *Cultures in Conflict: An Essay in the Philosophy of the Humanities.* Notre Dame: U of Notre Dame P, 1976.

Boyer Commission on Educating Undergraduates in the Research University. *Reinventing Undergraduate Education: A Blueprint for America's Research Universities.* New York: SUNY Stony Brook, 1998. 7 August 2001. <http://naples.cc.sunysb.edu/Pres/boyer.nsf>.

Brush, Stephen. "Should the History of Science be Rated X?" *Science* 22 March, 1974: 183.

Crombie, A.C., ed. *Scientific Change.* New York: Heinemann, 1963.

Frankl, Viktor. "Reductionism and Nihilism." *Beyond Reductionism.* Ed. A. Koestler and J.R. Smythies. New York: Macmillan, 1968.

Gross, Paul and Norman Leavitt. *Higher Superstition: The Academic Left and its Quarrels With Science.* Baltimore: Johns Hopkins Press, 1994.

Kimball, Bruce R. *Orators and Philosophers: A History of the Idea of Liberal Education.* New York: Teacher's College Press, 1986.

Koestler, A. and J.R. Smythies, eds. *Beyond Reductionism.* New York: Macmillan, 1968.

Kuhn, Thomas. *The Structure of Scientific Revolutions*, 2nd ed. Chicago: U of Chicago P, 1970.

MacIntyre, Alasdair. *Three Rival Versions of Moral Inquiry.* London: Duckworth, 1990.

Sargent, R. ed. *Francis Bacon, Selected Philosophical Works.* Indianapolis: Hackett, 1999.

Sokal, Alan. "Transgressing the Boundaries: Towards a Transformative Hermeneutics of Quantum Gravity." *Social Text* 46/47 (1996): 217-52.

Sokal, Alan. *Lingua Franca* May/June (1996): 62-64.

Wertheim, Margaret. "After the Double Helix: Unraveling the Mysteries of the State of Being." *New York Times* 13 Apr. 2004: D3.

Plato's *Crito* and the Development of Community

David Shiner
Shimer College

When casting about for a philosophical work that can profitably help foster a sense of community, Plato's *Crito* is at first glance an unlikely choice. As the middle dialogue of three dealing with Socrates' trial and death, it is in some sense the least capable of standing alone, that is, apart from the dialogues detailing the events that purportedly preceded and followed it (*Apology* and *Phaedo*). The dialogue itself includes only two persons, a far cry from more heavily populated ones such as *Symposium* and *Republic*, in which the presence of a sort of community is always evident. And while the theme of the *Crito* is not easy to state concisely, it certainly is not the nature of community. Nevertheless I have chosen to discuss the *Crito* because, in my experience as a seminar leader at Shimer College, it has proven fruitful in illuminating certain aspects of the nature of community in ways that no other Platonic dialogue, and perhaps no other written work, has proven able to do.

The aspects of the *Crito* that seem to me to foster community, or at least to encourage reflection about it, are the following:

1. The cooperative examination and critical appraisal of an approach to ethical concerns that was widely regarded as common sense then and is widely regarded the same way now;
2. The exploration of ideas in conjunction with others, rather than in isolation (as against, say, the work and explicit ideas of Descartes); and,
3. The construction of an argument on behalf of community rather than the (apparent) good of the individual.

All of these points, it should be noted, would be of limited value if simply related to students in a lecture format. A seminar, the form of which mirrors the Platonic dialogues, helps to facilitate the process of having the less obvious messages and implications, the so-called "hidden curriculum," influence the participants.

Students who enter the seminar room having just read the *Crito* for the first time are likely to have been most affected by Socrates' final claim, that the laws of the state must be obeyed regardless what they decree. As this point of view is hardly conformable to the beliefs of contemporary Americans of any political persuasion, particularly young ones, it is important that the arguments that support it be studied and considered with care. However, it is even more important that full discussion of its meaning and merit be deferred until the earlier portions of the *Crito* have been reckoned with.

In the early part of the dialogue, Socrates' friend Crito presents a series of arguments to the effect that Socrates should escape from prison immediately. These arguments are of various kinds; some are quasi-rational, while others are based on expediency since the time for escaping, or at least escaping easily, will soon pass. Socrates replies to all these as follows:

> My dear Crito, I thank you for your warm feelings toward me, assuming they are justified. If they are not, the stronger they are, the harder they will be to deal with. Therefore we ought to consider whether it is right to do as you say. (46b)

With these words, Socrates changes the focus of the discussion. The issue is not to be what is expedient, what appears right; it's what *is* right. Crito, committed for the moment to views that he believes are rationally-based but which, when subjected to the rigor and vigor of Socratic questioning, will turn out to be nothing but rationalizations, agrees to this exploration, believing that his point of view will be justified by means of the inquiry.

The unfolding of discourse, like the building of community itself, takes time. This is a frequent lesson of the Platonic dialogues. In the *Apology*, for example, Socrates notes that the Athenian trial system does not allow sufficient time for the development and influence of rational argumentation, concluding, "I cannot convince you, because we have had so little time for discussion" (*Apology* 37a). Similarly, Crito's impatience hinders his ability to engage fully in Socrates' responses to his arguments during the first half of the *Crito*. At one point he (Crito) states, "I think that what you say is good, Socrates, but I wish you would consider what we should do" (48d). In our world, as in ancient Athens, "doers" are often applauded for acting quickly and decisively, but rational discourse and reflection do not always confirm that such approval is justified. Socrates bases his praxis on logos, not the reverse. This means that Crito's impatience will have to be set aside while his conversation with Socrates takes its course. As witnesses to this process, students, like Crito, are gently guided to understand that patience is a cardinal virtue with respect to rational discourse.

As the dialogue proceeds, Crito comes increasingly to accept arguments that undermine his position that Socrates should escape prison at once, or for that matter at all. At one point, Socrates asks Crito whether their previous agreements that death was preferable to dishonor, agreements at which they had arrived when neither of them was in a position of having to act on the basis of them, are still valid.

> Do we still say that one must never intentionally do wrong, or does it depend on the circumstances? Is it true, as we have often agreed in the past, that wrongdoing can never be good or honorable? Or have we disavowed all our previous convictions in these last few days? Can you and I at our age, Crito, have spent all these years in serious discussions without realizing that we were no better than two children? (49a)

Elsewhere, Socrates wonders aloud whether his perspective on this matter "was right before the question of my death arose, but now . . . is a mistaken persistence in a point of view that was really irresponsible nonsense" (46d). Such passages raise the issue of whether ethics are situational or absolutistic. Socrates consistently argues in favor of the latter position. As Crito shares this view, at least in his rational moments, he is duty-bound not to disagree with Socrates here.

And it would be difficult for the rest of us to do so either, at least without serious reflection and soul-searching. The argument of the *Crito* is often juxtaposed against that of Thoreau in his "Essay on Civil Disobedience," long a popular treatise with the younger set. However, by noting that an argument in favor of disobedience in this case would confirm the charge of Socrates' accusers that he is hostile to the laws (53c), Socrates implicitly asks each of us to consider whether the practice of civil disobedience under any circumstances is motivated as nobly as we might wish to believe. Our contemporary inclinations toward individualism, relativism, subjectivism, and the like make this concern even more urgent than in Socrates' day.

Despite such inclinations, students—at least my students—are normally inclined to side with Socrates up to this point in the dialogue. They regard themselves as ethical people, and they tend to believe, at least in theory, that one should do the right thing regardless of circumstances. Even those who opine that Socrates should have escaped from prison because he was wronged (or for whatever reason) tend to believe this because of their sympathy for him, even if that sympathy is wrongly motivated (wrongly, at least, by the terms of Socrates' own views) by their belief that life is superior to death.

Much sympathy for Socrates' approach is spurred among my students by his question to Crito: "[H]aving suffered harm, is it just or unjust to inflict harm in return?" (49a). Phrasing the question in this way augurs in favor of a response that retribution is unjust, and this is indeed how Crito replies. Subsequently and more crucially, Socrates asks him to consider carefully whether he really believes this to be true. And well he might, since Crito's exhortation that Socrates escape from prison implicitly assumes either the very opposite or else that Crito is not really concerned about justice.

This argument, as Plato makes clear, is not just about Socrates and Crito as individuals. As Socrates says in asking his friend to consider this particular matter:

> Now be careful, Crito, that in making these single admissions you do not end up stating something contrary to your real beliefs. I know that there are and always will be few people who think like this, and that consequently there can be no agreement on principle between those who think so and those who do not. Each must always feel contempt when they observe each other's decisions. (49d)

This mode of speech enlarges the discourse of the *Crito* to the human community, implicitly entreating each reader to consider whether any community to which he or she belongs is a just one. Each reader must come to grips with this question for her- or himself, realizing that the terms of the debate as posed by Socrates allow of no gray area. These terms build a boundary around the community of the just, the members of which will inevitably be scorned by those who are not wholly dedicated to righteousness and who therefore are not members of any community worthy of the name. Here my students are divided. Some, like Socrates, see this distinction as acceptable, even noble; others, like Crito, are less certain.

The great coda of the argument, however, is one that my students—like, I believe, most students—have difficulty accepting. This is the point at which Socrates invokes the authority and voice of the laws of Athens. These laws, as Plato has them argue on their own behalf, almost literally brought him into the world. They sanctioned the marriage of his mother and father, thus legitimizing him as a human being. They created a context through which he could have a name, an address, a very state of being. He has never had any quarrel with them; or, if he has, he has never acted on the basis of it (for example, by leaving the city-state). Would it not be presumptuous and ungrateful for him to decide that any of the city's laws is unworthy, and hypocritical and opportunistic for him to decide that the law that is least worthy— that is, the one he will implicitly be violating through his actions should he choose to escape—happens to be the very one that would presumably harm him most?

This argument speaks forcefully to the nature of citizenship, one important form of membership in a community. Students might not accept it, and most of mine do not, but if they are even passingly attentive they must come to grips with it. Some will state that it is clear from the *Apology* that the decision to put Socrates to death was unjust. It quickly becomes evident, however, that Socrates' claim, both there and in the *Crito,* is that human beings can act unjustly, but the laws cannot (for example, 54c).

The discourse of the laws of Athens augurs against the subjectivist inclinations of most citizens from both Socrates' time and our own. The laws universalize Socrates' impending decision in a proto-Kantian manner, insisting that he imagine a choice to escape from prison under the present circumstances as if it were to be universalized into an ethical maxim. The result would clearly be anarchy, and, despite the accusations of his accusers, Socrates notes, "Who would want to live in a city without laws?" (53a). Socrates' position is that escaping would contradict his status as the progeny of the state that made him who he is. It is, he claims, through membership in such a community that we become who we are. We disregard this verity on pain of hypocrisy. Most of us, however, do disregard it, especially when it suits what we take to be our current purposes. Socrates does not.

To the extent that this line of reasoning is persuasive to my predominantly leftist students, it is so in part because it is not a "my country right or wrong" argument, at least not predominantly so. Plato goes to great pains to indicate that Socrates has demonstrated his loyalty to Athens in many ways, such as the fact that, although he has on occasion offered criticisms of the Athenian city-state and could have freely departed at any time, he in fact ventured outside the city walls less frequently "than the lame and the blind and other cripples" (53a). He has professed himself pleased with some of the city's laws and has been compliant with the rest; he willingly participated in a trial that, although stacked against him, committed him tacitly to the assumption that its laws were worthy of his obedience. He could have used his powers of persuasion to argue for changes in any of his city's laws; he chose not to do so. He is therefore a true citizen of Athens, not contingently, but in an essential way, a way that defines his very being, and defines it far more than is true of most of his fellow citizens. His escape would be analogous to a branch attempting to cut off the tree that spawned it. It would be a small contribution, but a contribution nonetheless, to the destruction of the community that gave Socrates not only his life but also his sustenance, in every sense of the word.

In our seminar classes at Shimer, we consider the creation and nurturance of community, a community of discourse, to be of paramount importance. To be sure, our seminar groups are but temporary communities; but they are also ones in which some of the finest aspects of communitarian life can be practiced, and students at Shimer are strongly encouraged in this direction. They are expected to read carefully and discourse intelligently, and they generally do so. They consider issues such as justice and goodness in a context in which their considerations are tested with concern for truth and respect for their fellows, and they are expected to act in accordance with those values, both inside and outside of class. They form, at least in their best moments, something like an ideal community, although admittedly a limited one. I know of no better model for such a community than the

Platonic dialogues, and no better dialogue for such modeling than the *Crito*.

Works Cited
Plato. *Five Dialogues: Euthyphro, Apology, Crito, Meno, Phaedo.* 2nd ed. Trans. G. M. A. Grube. Indianapolis: Hackett Publishing Company, 1997.

Augustine's Intellectual Conversion

Richard M. Liddy
Seton Hall University

Most prominent in the *Confessions* are Augustine's moral and religious strivings and the moment of his religious conversion in the garden in Milan in August of 386. But equally present in Augustine's story are his philosophical journey and what Bernard Lonergan called his "intellectual conversion," which took place in the spring and summer of 386 and which he describes in book VII of the *Confessions*. This paper will focus on teaching the *Confessions* in such a way as to give sufficient weight to this great "change of mind" that prepared the way for his later religious and moral conversion.

But what is intellectual conversion? If we are going to use this as a heuristic for understanding a great theme in the *Confessions*, we need to have some idea of what we are talking about. In the first section of this paper we will present an example from learning a science and some account of the meaning of this event; in the second section we will show this change of mind exemplified in the *Confessions*.

The physicist Freeman Dyson once described the process involved in his students learning quantum mechanics. It involves three stages.

> The student begins by learning the tricks of the trade. He learns how to make calculations in quantum mechanics and get the right answers . . . . To learn the mathematics of the subject and to learn how to use it takes

about six months. This is the first stage in learning quantum mechanics, and it is comparatively easy and painless. The second stage comes when the student begins to worry because he does not understand what he has been doing. He worries because he has no clear physical picture in his head. He gets confused in trying to arrive at a physical explanation for each of the mathematical tricks he has been taught. He works very hard and gets discouraged because he does not seem able to think clearly. This second stage often lasts six months or longer, and it is strenuous and unpleasant. Then, quite unexpectedly, the third stage begins. The student suddenly says to himself, "I understand quantum mechanics," or rather he says, "I understand now that there really isn't anything to be understood." (259-260)

In other words, the student comes to understand that there really isn't anything to be understood in the "clear physical pictures" she had been seeking. Certainly the student has been learning something—quantum mechanics—but at the same time she comes to understand that that learning involves "unlearning something," that is, one's spontaneous anticipations about reality. And that can be a painful process. In a more contemporary language, one ceases to consider knowing to be merely experiencing or having representative images, and one comes to realize that genuine knowledge consists in accurate understanding and true judgment. Realizing this—coming to understand one's own understanding—is what Bernard Lonergan calls intellectual conversion. For, as he puts it,

> some form of naïve realism seems to appear utterly unquestionable to very many. As soon as they begin to speak of knowing, of objectivity, of reality, there crops up the assumption that all knowing must be something like looking. To be liberated from that blunder, to discover the self-transcendence proper to the human process of coming to know, is to break often long-ingrained habits of thought and speech. It is to acquire the mastery in one's own house that is to be had only when one knows precisely what one is doing when one is knowing. It is a conversion, a new beginning, a fresh start. It opens the way to ever further clarifications and developments. (239-240)

Elsewhere Lonergan notes that one has not made such a breakthrough yet if one has no clear memory of its "startling strangeness" (22).

Now what does this have to do with Augustine's *Confessions*? Well, in the *Confessions*, it is clear that Augustine does have a clear memory of such a startling breakthrough, and it is chiefly recounted in book 7, but its echo can be heard throughout the *Confessions*. According to his great biographer, Peter Brown, Augustine could not have told us such an interesting story about his life if he had not had at hand a language which helped him understand his own story and to tell it so well. A significant contribution to that language, as he tells us in book 7, came from some "books of the Platonists" lent to him by an acquaintance in the spring of 386. As Brown puts it:

> For the Neo-Platonists provided [Augustine] with the one essential tool for any serious autobiography; they had given him a theory of the dynamics of the soul that made sense of his experience. (95)

One element in those "dynamics of the soul" was Augustine's radical desire to understand. At the age of nineteen, buffeted by the winds of desire, Augustine happened upon Cicero's *Hortensius*, a book since lost to history. Through that book he discovered in himself a new dimension of desire, the desire to understand.

> Quite definitely it changed the direction of my mind . . . . Suddenly all the vanity I had hoped in I saw as worthless, and with an incredible intensity of desire I longed after inward wisdom. I had begun that journey upwards by which I was to return to You...The one thing that delighted me in Cicero's exhortation was that I should love, and seek, and win, and hold, and embrace, not this or that philosophical school but Wisdom itself, whatever it might be. (*Confessions* III.4)

What the *Hortensius* represented for Augustine was a disinterested search for the truth, a desire that remained in him through the years and kept him moving from one school of philosophy to another: from Manichaeism to Academic skepticism and beyond. Having eventually become disillusioned with the fantastic myths of the Manichees and the quite evident lack of erudition of the sect's chief exponent, Faustus, Augustine was of a more or less skeptical frame of mind when in the spring of 386 he happened upon "some books of the Platonists," probably the books of Plotinus and some by his student Porphyry. These books were "packed with thought," (libri quidem pleni), and they produced in him a "conflagration" (*Contra Academicos* 2, 2, 5).

And what did Augustine find in these books that they had such a massive effect on him? First of all, they explicitly "turned him inward" toward his own conscious self. "Being admonished by all this to return to myself, I entered into my own depths . . ." (*Confessions* VII.10).

Secondly, under the influence of this reading he began to think of "spirit" in its own terms and not as understood in bodily ways. He came to realize that his chief intellectual obstacle had been his need to imaginatively "picture" things which cannot strictly speaking be pictured—whether his own mind, his own being, reality, evil or God.

For example, right from the first pages of the *Confessions*, Augustine reflects on the nature of the divine and how it transcends any images he could construct. How could he call on God, for example, he asks, to "come into him," if it is indeed true that God is everywhere and in all? Eventually he recounts his discovery that all his understandings of the divine had been clouded by his imagination.

> Though I did not even then think of You under the shape of a human body, yet I could not but think of You as some corporeal substance, occupying all space, whether infused in the world, or else diffused through infinite space beyond the world. (VII.1)

> When I desired to think of my God, I could not think of him save as a bodily magnitude—for it seemed to me that what was not such was nothing at all: this indeed was the principal and practically the sole cause of my inevitable error. (V.10)

In other words, what Augustine thought was God he came to discover was not God. Augustine even thought of evil as a type of bodily substance. For a long time he had been troubled by the nature of evil, and the Manicheans had influenced him to think of evil as some kind of "bodily substance," another principle opposed to the good God.

> I did not know that evil has no being of its own but is only an absence of good, so that it simply is not. How indeed should I see this, when the sight of my eyes saw no deeper than bodies and the sight of my soul no deeper than the images of bodies? (III.7)

> In my ignorance I thought of evil not simply as some kind of substance, but actually as a bodily substance, because I had not learned to think of mind save as a more subtle body, extended in space. (V.10)

The philosophical issue, as he slowly began to realize, was the character of his own mind.

> My mind was in search of such images as the forms of my eye was accustomed to see; and I did not realize that the mental act by which I formed these images, was not itself a bodily image. (VII.1)

Slowly, Augustine began to believe not only in the unseen, but also in the totally different character of such reality, reality mediated to us by language and words.

> I began to consider the countless things I believed which I had not seen, or which had happened with me not there—so many things in the history of nations, so many facts about places and cities, which I had never seen, so many things told me by friends, by doctors, by this man, by that man; and unless we accepted these things, we should do nothing at all in this life. Most strongly of all it struck me how firmly and unshakably I believed that I was born of a particular father and mother, which I could not possibly know unless I believed it on the word of others. (VI.5)

Lonergan would speak of this as Augustine's discovery of the world mediated by meaning, that is, by acts of understanding, judging and believing. Such a world goes far beyond the world of immediacy: of sights and sounds, touches and smells, tastes and feelings. It is a world in which Augustine had lived since he had learned how to speak, but it was a world he was, at the age of thirty-one, just coming to recognize. This world mediated by meaning is a fragile world, for besides fact, there is fiction. Consequently, there was his growing ability to think in terms of *"veritas,"* or true reality, rooted in God.

Centuries later, Bernard Lonergan, writing in a scientific context, will write of the similarity of this transition in Augustine's life to the transition that is implied in doing modern science—the transition to which Dyson's students were exposed.

> St. Augustine of Hippo narrates that it took him years to make the discovery that the name, real, might have a different connotation from the name, body. Or, to bring the point nearer home, one might say that it has taken modern science four centuries to make the discovery that the objects of its inquiry need not be imaginable entities moving through imaginable processes in an imaginable space-time. The fact that a Plato attempted to communicate through his dialogues, the fact that an Augustine eventually learnt from the writers whom, rather generally, he refers to as Platonists, has lost its antique flavor and its apparent irrelevance to the modern mind. Even before Einstein and Heisenberg it

was clear enough that the world described by scientists was strangely different from the world depicted by artists and inhabited by men of common sense. But it was left to twentieth-century physicists to envisage the possibility that the objects of their science were to be reached only by severing the umbilical cord that tied them to the maternal imagination of man. (15)

If Dyson's students had spent as much time thinking about themselves and their own spirit as they did about quantum mechanics, they might have had as startling and strange experience as Augustine did in the spring and summer of the year 386.

Works Cited

Augustine. *Confessions*. Trans. F. J. Sheed. New York: Sheed and Ward, 1942.

---. *The Fathers of the Church: Writings of Saint Augustine*. 1. Ed. Ludwig Schopp. New York: Cima Publishing Co., 1948.

---. *Contra Academicos. The Fathers of the Church, Writings of Saint Augustine*. Vol. 1. Ed. Ludwig Schopp. New York: Cima Publishing Co., 1948.

Brown, Peter. *Augustine of Hippo*. Berkeley: U of California P, 1969.

Dyson, Freeman. "Innovation in Physics." *Physics*. Eds. Samuel Rapport and Helen Wright. New York: Washington Square Press, 1965. 259-260

Lonergan, Bernard. "Insight: An Essay on Human Understanding" *Collected Works of Bernard Lonergan*. Ed. Frederick Crowe and Robert Doran. Vol. 3. U of Toronto P, 1992.

---. "Method in Catholic Theology." *Method: Journal of Lonergan Studies* 10.1 (1992): 1-23.

---. *Method in Theology*. Toronto: U of Toronto P, 1979.

---. *Topics in Education. Lectures on The Philosophy of Education. Collected Works of Bernard Lonergan*. Ed. Frederick Crowe and Robert Doran. Vol. 10. U of Toronto P, 1993.

Views of Community

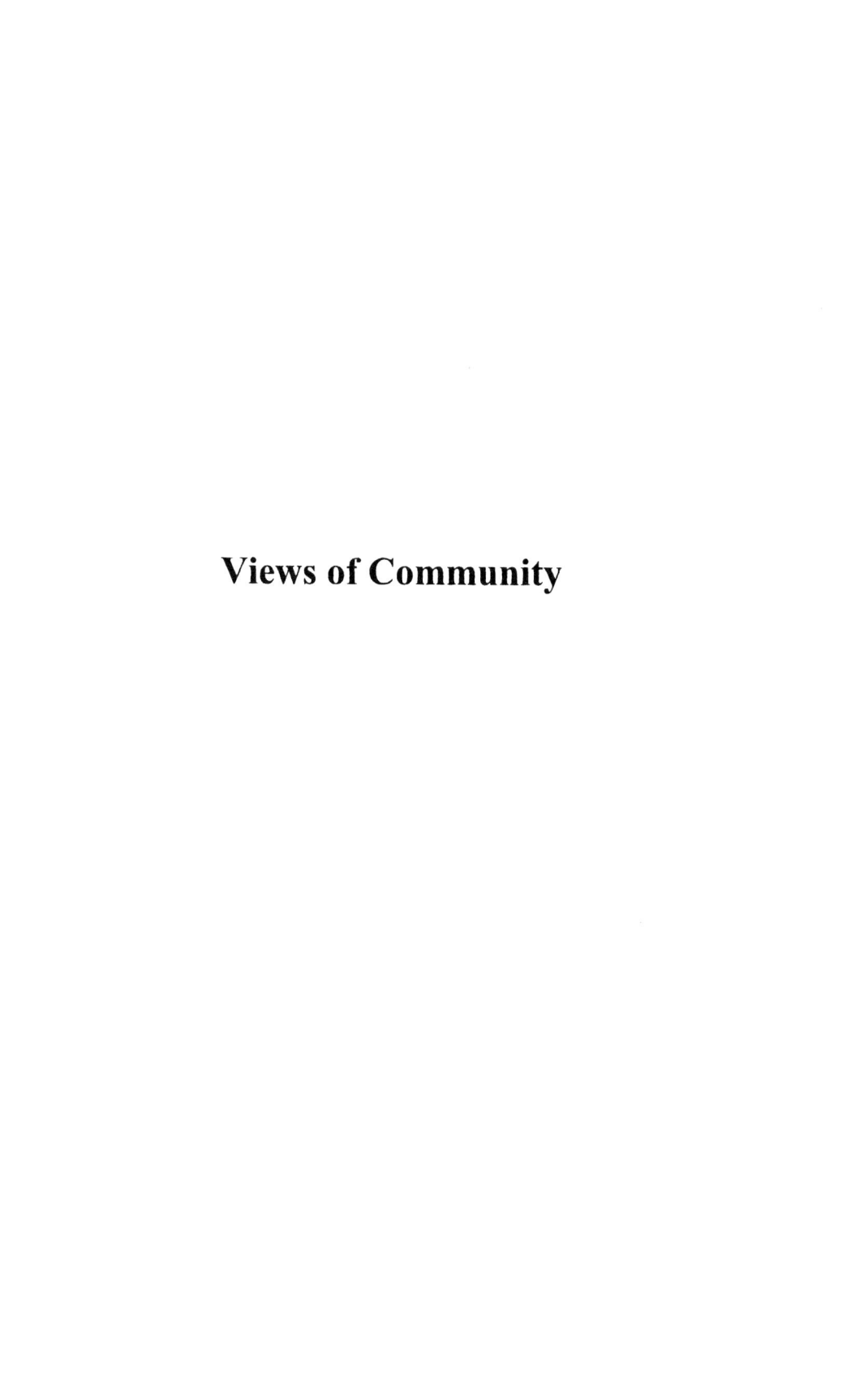

Beowulf: The Other Epic

Christine Cornell
St. Thomas University
Fredericton, Canada

Typical course booklists and previous ACTC programs attest to the infrequent use of the Anglo-Saxon epic, *Beowulf*, in core courses. In a way this is understandable: after some combination of the *Iliad*, the *Odyssey*, and the *Aeneid*, a teacher might well feel that enough time has been given to the epic and to the heroic ethos. Since, I suspect, few would argue that *Beowulf* is not worthy of consideration, I will make a case for its regular inclusion in the core. Much can be said in favor of the poem, but a worthwhile starting point is to consider where *Beowulf* stands in relation to the great conversation of Western thought.

Through historical circumstance, the role of *Beowulf* in the conversation has been rather one-sided. For many centuries the poem dropped from sight because of its existence in a single manuscript and because the language of that manuscript was inaccessible. *Beowulf* has been available both in the original language and in numerous translations only since the 1800s. During this relatively short time, its impact has been felt in poetry, fiction, film, and even comics. Nevertheless, since its recovery the poem, in academic terms, has remained largely in the domain of language and literature scholars. However, as in the case of the centuries of enforced silence, I would argue the current academic home of *Beowulf* is more a product of circumstance than necessity.

The *Beowulf* poet, for all that he lived on the cold outer edge of eighth-century Europe, was—like his culture—very much a part of the conversation stretching back to classical antiquity. The poem is well situated to provide us with a voice from the often-neglected centuries between Augustine and Dante. Obviously, historical coverage alone would hardly make a case for the poem, but *Beowulf* takes up an essential strand of the concerns of the age: how is an eighth- or tenth-century Christian to understand and evaluate the pre-Christian thought of his or her ancestors? The question is not simply one of historical interest for either Aquinas, the *Beowulf* poet, or us. The *Beowulf* poet wrestles with what is true in the pre-Christian understanding of ideas such as courage, generosity, honor, loyalty, leadership, mortality, and fate.

A reader of *Beowulf* will find much that is reminiscent of the classical epics, including references to the *Aeneid*. However, for all that the poet is often sympathetic in his treatment of Beowulf's world, it is not the poet's world. Critics are divided on the ultimate outcome of the encounter. Some see the poem as nostalgic praise for the virtues of the pre-Christian past. Others see it as a Christian condemnation of pagan pride and meaningless heroics. Still others see the poet as attempting a—sometimes more, sometimes less successful—synthesis of pagan and Christian values. More attention to this subject would be desirable, but what is clear is that the poem engages with these issues in a compelling and thoughtful manner. A brief and necessarily incomplete look at the poem's treatment of fate and human mortality will hopefully suffice to demonstrate the kinds of questions raised by *Beowulf* and the discussions it can generate.

I would like to offer a starting point that draws on a work from the same period as the poem. In his *A History of the English Church and People*, Bede describes King Edwin's deliberation before his conversion to Christianity. A member of the king's court offers this advice:

> Your Majesty, when we compare the present life of man on earth with that time of which we have no knowledge, it seems to me like the swift flight of a single sparrow through the banqueting-hall where you are sitting at dinner on a winter's day with your thanes and counsellors. In the midst there is a comforting fire to warm the hall; outside, the storms of winter rain or snow are raging. This sparrow flies swiftly in through one door of the hall, and out through another. While he is inside, he is safe from the winter storms; but after a few moments of comfort, he vanishes from sight into the wintry world from which he came. Even so, man appears on earth for a little while; but of what went before this life or of what follows, we know nothing. Therefore, if this new teaching has

brought more certain knowledge, it seems only right that we should follow it. (127)

Beowulf opens on a similar note.

The first major episode of the poem is the story of Beowulf, a hero of the royal house of the Geats coming to the aid of the Danish King Hrothgar and ridding Hrothgar's kingdom of the monster Grendel. The poem opens, however, with a brief description of the life of Hrothgar's great-grandfather, Scyld Shefing. Scyld is presented as the epitome of a good king, who rises to this position from having been a foundling from the sea. When he dies at the end of a long life, Scyld is placed in a boat with his burial treasures and returned to the sea. The narrator observes, "Men under heaven's / shifting skies, though skilled in counsel, / cannot say surely who unshipped that cargo" (49-51). As with King Edwin's advisor, for the characters of *Beowulf* there is no certain knowledge of what comes "before this life or of what follows": for them there is only Wyrd—fate, or literally "what happens."

However, Wyrd is not given the final word in the poem, since the narrator of *Beowulf* is decidedly Christian. The narrator provides a providential view which stands above Wyrd. For instance, in discussing the men killed by Grendel, the narrator observes

> more would have gone
> had not the God overseeing us, and the resolve of a man,
> stood against that wyrd. The Wielder guided then
> the dealings of mankind, as He does even now.
> A mind that seeks to understand and grasp this
> is therefore best. Both bad and good,
> and much of both, must be borne in a lifetime
> spent on this earth in these anxious days. (1054-1061)

Beowulf, like the *Iliad*, raises questions about free will and fate. In both poems the actions of the greatest heroes are set against the notion of fate. The *Beowulf* poet, however, takes the further step of placing this discussion against a Christian background where fate must give way to the providential designs of the Creator. In the classroom this creates the opportunity to compare the concepts of fate and providence as they are worked out within a single work.

In addition to the mystery that surrounds life, Bede's story of the sparrow also speaks to the briefness of life, as the sparrow spends scant moments in the brightness of the hall before returning to the darkness.

Reflections on the briefness of life and the realities of mortality run throughout *Beowulf*. At times the *Beowulf* poet employs a kind of double focus: one moment we watch characters and events through the lens of the heroic ethos, at another we are offered a Christian viewpoint.

The pre-Christian outlook seems to allow the poet the opportunity to consider the problems of mortality, kingship, and political rule from a secular perspective. These problems are raised early in the poem when the narrator suggests

> in youth an atheling should so use his virtue,
> give with a free hand while in his father's house,
> that in old age, when enemies gather,
> established friends shall stand by him
> and serve him gladly. (20-24)

However, it is quickly evident that this strategy is far from perfect. Hrothgar, who by all accounts has been a good and generous ruler, nevertheless finds himself unable to protect his community as he ages. In the end, Hrothgar's hall is saved from Grendel by the outsider, Beowulf, not through the actions of Hrothgar's own warriors.

The inevitability, in the natural course of things, of aging and death is driven home by the *Beowulf* poet in his striking use of the rapid passage of time. Beowulf, the young hero, returns home triumphant from his rescue of Hrothgar, and within nine lines, Beowulf's own lord and his lord's heir are dead, while Beowulf has been made king and has ruled for half a century.

Like Hrothgar, Beowulf has ruled well, but also like Hrothgar, Beowulf and his people must face a monster. As Beowulf, now old, prepares to do battle with a deadly dragon, he takes with him eleven warriors. For all that Beowulf has been a kind and generous ruler, his warriors, with one exception, fail to stand by him. Between Beowulf and the one loyal young warrior, Wiglaf, they are able to kill the dragon, but Beowulf is also killed. Wiglaf bitterly predicts the destruction of the Geats will follow— not so much from Beowulf's death, as from the faithlessness of his men. The idea that good rule while a king is young will stand him in good stead when he is old is shown to be incomplete: Wiglaf does stand by his lord; the dragon is destroyed, but the majority fail their king, and he is killed defending them.

Beowulf's death is inescapable, and the poet seems to suggest the subsequent decay of Beowulf's kingdom is similarly unavoidable. That said, in a world riven by tribal warfare and blood feuds, the fifty good years under Beowulf's rule is not a negligible accomplishment. However, from Hrothgar in the beginning to Beowulf at the conclusion, the poem reminds us of the inevitable loss of strength and power which every hero—and man—who lives to see old age must endure. In the face of this inevitability, the noble and heroic efforts of the greatest rulers are unable to ensure the future safety and success of their people. The *Beowulf* poet suggests that this reality, perhaps more than any other, is a bond shared by his heroic pre-Christian ancestors and his own age.

At the same time, from the perspective of the Christian narrator, the fate of the people, heroes, rulers, and kingdoms is finally in God's hands not man's. As Hrothgar observes,

> It is wonderful to recount
> how in his magnanimity the Almighty God
> deals out wisdom, dominion, and lordship
> among mankind. The Master of all things
> will sometimes allow the soul of a man
> of well-known kindred to wander in delight:
> He will grant him earth's bliss in his own homeland,
> the sway of the fortress-city of his people,
> and will give him to rule regions of the world,
> wide kingdoms: he cannot imagine,
> in his unwisdom, that an end will come. (1723-1733)

Hrothgar continues, "ultimately the end must come, / the frail house of flesh must crumble / and fall at its hour" (1752-54). This awareness of the impermanence of all human things runs through the entire poem.

Beowulf offers reflections on critical questions: given the impermanence of things of human making, how are we to live? How are we to establish and maintain human community? What makes a good ruler? What place is there for human action in a world ruled by change and time or by the Christian God? As an early Christian looking back and drawing on the ideas and stories of the pre-Christian Germanic world, the *Beowulf* poet creates a poem ideally suited to resume its place in the great conversation.

Works Cited

Bede. *A History of the English Church and People*. Trans. Leo Sherley-Price. Harmondsworth, Middlesex: Penguin, 1968.

Beowulf: A Verse Translation. Trans. Michael Alexander. London: Penguin, 2001.

Montesquieu and the Problematic Character of Modern Citizenship

Matthew Davis
St. John's College, Santa Fe

Note: Let me begin by saying that this paper emerged out of a St. John's College faculty seminar, which we held in order to discover whether we could find a place for Montesquieu in the readings of the junior year. The junior year seminar at St. John's is devoted largely to readings from Enlightenment figures, among whom Montesquieu occupies an unusual place, for although he may be a promoter of the Enlightenment, he also has an unflinching awareness of its shortcomings.

The topic of our panel is "The Duty of Citizenship." If we begin from where we are—living in an ever-expanding commercial republic that recognizes and embraces as one of its fundamental principles the protection and promotion of individual liberty—then in a moment's reflection we can see that this is a very complicated topic. For if it is a fundamental fact that we have the liberty to pursue happiness—and in the commercial republic this pursuit is largely understood as the pursuit and amassing of material wealth—then we discover that in the course of this pursuit, it is unclear precisely how far our duties to others extend. Let me offer a couple of illustrations of what I mean. Recently I sold a house. In striving to get the "best deal," it became clear to me that my real estate agent was treating the potential buyer—who in other circumstances might have been a friend—as an enemy. She used every manipulative tactic she could legally use in order to gain the best price, and, above all, until she made the sale she made sure that she kept the buyer and the seller apart, so that no bond could form between us. She had been a former teacher, and at one point she compared real estate sales to a "state of nature." (Nevertheless, in all her dealings, she was extremely nice, and never once stopped smiling.) Or one could cite our use of the automobile, which illustrates even more radically our blatant preference for individual liberty over our duties as citizens to our fellow citizens. We go on driving—with larger and larger vehicles, I might add—and disregard the huge number of our fellow citizens who are killed by cars every year. Winston Churchill notes in this regard that the ancients would have been appalled by such a lack of concern for their fellow citizens. And he noted it, by the way, in 1930, when the number of traffic deaths was a fraction of what it is today. As these examples suggest, the legally prescribed duties that we have toward our fellows in the modern commercial republic are minimal, so minimal that they barely mask the thinly veiled state of indifference, or even enmity, that exists just below their surface. (They are also extremely obscure, by the way, as anyone who has ever sold a house or paid taxes knows.) Surely, one would think, our duties towards others are greater than this.

Montesquieu saw all of this centuries ago. In book 19, chapter 27 of *The Spirit of the Laws,* Montesquieu sketches a picture of modern England, a commercial republic whose chief principle is liberty, and which in many of its most important features looks very much like the United States today. He tells us, for example, that in such a republic "as each individual, always independent, would largely follow his own caprices and his fantasies, he would often change parties; he would abandon one and leave all his friends in order to bind himself to another in which he would find all his enemies; and often, in this nation, he could forget both the laws of friendship and those of hatred" (326). (Here again I am reminded of Churchill, who as some may recall famously changed parties.) Even more to the point, Montesquieu also says the following: "As the laws [in the modern commercial republic] would not be made for one individual more than another, each would regard himself as the monarch; the men in this nation would be confederates more than fellow citizens" (332). Far from being friends, the individuals in such a republic are not even citizens in the fullest sense; instead, they treat one another as though foreign policy were domestic policy, as though they were rival monarchs forming confederations with one another. In book 9 of *The Spirit of the Laws,* Montesquieu describes a confederation as a group of nations that comes together merely for defensive purposes. In order to maintain their alliance, they impose equal laws so that none of the confederated states will tyrannize over the others. Such is our lot, then, in the modern commercial republic. In order to promote the liberty to pursue our own happiness, we confederate with others for defensive purposes. Still, since down deep we also know that we are at odds even with our confederates, we distrust them, and we spend our lives in a constant state of agitation, always in need of greater personal security, of increasing our own personal wealth. (The way that mutual fund companies have promoted retirement plans, always playing on the fears about loss of security of those who are far wealthier than even my parents' generation could have dreamed, is a case in point.) As Montesquieu notes, "the people would be uneasy about their situation and would believe themselves in danger even at the safest moments" (326). Put another way, our situation forces us to become the *bourgeois,* to become people who, like my real estate agent, appear the paradigm of politeness and concern, while all the while using others—using those whom they merely call their fellow "citizens"—for their own gain.

So, those who feel ill at ease in the *bourgeois* atmosphere of the modern commercial republic, who realize that this atmosphere in its very character prevents them from fully realizing the profound duties that they feel toward their fellows, might wonder whether the modern commercial republic is all there is. Of course, if individual liberty and the right to pursue one's own version of happiness are fundamental facts, then the modern commercial state, in whatever form it may take, is also simply a fact of life. But are individual liberty and the modern commercial state genuine facts of life?

This is of course a much larger question than can be addressed here. My sense, though, is that at least at the outset of an investigation of it, Montesquieu can again be our guide. One of the strangest things about book 19 of *The Spirit of the Laws* is that just prior to his discussion of England, in the final chapter of that book, Montesquieu says the following: "We have seen how laws follow mores, let us now see how mores follow laws" (325). This sudden shift of course makes sense: if the unrestrained liberty of unformed individuals that underlies the modern commercial republic is the fundamental fact, then the imposition of laws with serious sanctions would be the prerequisite of any societal arrangement. But, as I have noted, Montesquieu contrasts this understanding with the ways of life that preceded the emergence of the modern commercial republic (or, better, the ways of life that preceded the emergence of the theory that gave rise to the emergence of the modern commercial republic). In these ways of life, the laws were deeply related to what Montesquieu calls the "general spirit" of a nation, a spirit which is formed by varying combinations of "climate, religion, laws, the maxims of government, examples of past things, mores, and manners" (310). In crafting the laws, Montesquieu argues, the wise legislator must pay close attention to this "general spirit." Moreover, Montesquieu shows particular interest in those legislators that have "confused" some of these things, as did, for example, Moses, when he "made a single code of laws and religion" (Montesquieu's footnote 16, 317), or as did the Chinese: ". . . they confused religion, laws, mores, and manners; all was morality, all was virtue" (318). Now, to be sure, Montesquieu calls the legislators who proceeded in this way "confused" and speaks of the liberty in the modern commercial republic as "true" (327), and perhaps in this way he indicates his preference for the modern commercial republic. But, unlike his great predecessors, Hobbes and Locke, Montesquieu does not present his thoughts in an argumentative, and somewhat rigid, theoretical form. Instead, he presents them in a very complicated, anecdotal manner, so complicated that many commentators have despaired of finding any rhyme or reason in *The Spirit of the Laws*. I wonder, though, whether Montesquieu's manner of presentation in book 19 (and the whole of the book), an example of which is his comment reversing the arrangement of laws and mores just prior to his discussion of the commercial republic, is in fact intended to lead his attentive readers first to recognize the presuppositions underlying the modern commercial republic and then, having the account of the preceding ways of life before them, to raise the question of whether or how those presuppositions have been established. In other words, Montesquieu's presentation invites his attentive readers to wonder whether the question of the best way of life has been answered in favor of the *bourgeois* life of the modern commercial republic, or whether this question is still open, and hence whether our longings for something better than this—for real friendship, for a liberal education that transcends the marketplace, for a genuine citizenship—might still be fulfilled.

Works Cited

Montesquieu, Charles de Secondat, baron de. *The Spirit of the Laws*. Trans. and eds. Anne Cohler, Basia Miller, and Harold Stone. Cambridge: Cambridge UP, 1989.

Kleos and Kitsch: Postcard Patriotism in Derek Walcott's *Omeros*

Joel Garza
University of Dallas

Epics traffic in nostalgia. From the regional details of *Iliad*'s catalogue of ships to Virgil's underworld catalogue of Roman heroes, epic poets, at some level, are driven by political influences. Nor is this nostalgia completely neutral. Homer candidly judges his listeners as far meaner men than his heroes (cf. the relative strengths of Hektor and Homer's listeners, *Iliad* 12.447). By contrast, Virgil raises the *fama* of his contemporaries to heroic heights—the exploits of Augustus depicted on Aeneas' shield give the Trojan exile great joy; Aeneas' destination by the white sow is presented as an underdeveloped outpost, not to reach its fullest glory until the now of Virgil's Rome. For *Omeros*, an epic poem and virtual love letter to the Caribbean island of St. Lucia, Derek Walcott is both as critical of his contemporaries as was Homer, yet as hopeful for and tender towards his birthplace as is Virgil. This ambiguous presentation of his island springs, in part, from the economic realities of his home. Whereas Homer's patriotic sentiments may have been dampened by various clan invasions, and Virgil's *pietas* may have suffered under the strain of the civil war and involuntary exile, neither had to endure St. Lucia's greatest foe, an enemy in some ways worse than the British or French empires. Homer and Virgil's heroes depend upon us for their life in glory; Walcott's depend upon us for their very livelihood. Unlike Homer's Greece or Virgil's Rome, St. Lucia suffers a daily assault, which ironically is also its lifeblood—tourists.

Tourism runs through Walcott's work. In the 1970 essay "What the Twilight Says," he admits that it is difficult to strike an artistic middle ground; at worst, his art is postcard verse, a well-meaning act of treachery, another minstrel show (8); at best, it is a poetry of absolution that becomes a "symbol of a carefree, accommodating culture, an adjunct to tourism" (7). Eight years later, he dramatized this difficult middle ground. In the play *Pantomime*, Harry Trewe, the white manager of a decrepit hotel, enlists Jackson Philip, his black servant, to help him stage *Robinson Crusoe* for his customers (or more accurately, in the hopes that they will get customers). Trewe, the manager, jokingly suggests that they trade roles—that is, the manager will play Friday and the servant Crusoe. In the rehearsal for this satire, however, this black Crusoe improvises a Thursday that prevents the white Friday from entering the drama. Walcott demonstrates in this farce the economic limitations placed on art—a true peripety, a genuine reversal that debases both figures and hurts the white people (cf. 111), which ultimately hurts both manager and servant. Economic survival, in this drama, depends upon keeping it light, which unfortunately locks both men in a mutually degrading if financially viable stasis.

Nor is tourism always a drama between the self-debased local and the patronizing visitor. Indeed, why reduce this presentation to the vocabulary of tourism; why not cast it in more eternal poetic terms of travel, journey, and adventure? In a 1985 interview, Derek Walcott speaks from both perspectives, praising his island, not as a poetic subject, or as another Eden, as he often does, but as a luxurious destination for all the weary: "People who come out . . . from the cities and continents go through a process of being recultured. What they encounter here, if they surrender to their seeing, has a lot to teach them, first of all the proven adaptability of races living next to each other . . . . And then also in the erasure of the idea of history . . . . There is a continual sense of motion in the Caribbean . . . . The size of time is larger . . . . We don't live so much by the clock" (108). St. Lucia illumines and heals much for her visitors. And for Walcott we are a world of visitors; few of *Omeros*' characters are local: from the British expatriates, to the descendants of the slave trade, from the Native Americans on their Trail of Tears, to the reimagined Homer shopping his poem around London, from the time-traveling Achille to our narrator himself, more frequent flyer than native son.

These post/colonial realities and depictions notwithstanding, tourism pervades this poem in a way that it never has in Walcott's work. Indeed, the reader's first view of St. Lucia is through the eyes of vacationers. Before introducing St. Lucia properly—its history, its natural beauty—Walcott opens *Omeros* with a charming local fisherman, Philoctete, entertaining tourists. This smiling guide displays his wound for these visitors' cameras. From a young age, St. Lucian boys brave the churning wakes of luxury liners, fighting with one another over coins that tourists toss overboard (73); this diving for pennies also comes up in George Lamming's novel *In the Castle of My Skin*, depicting his upbringing in and leaving of Barbados (116). Helen, a symbol for and the greatest flower of the island's beauty, far from the privileged place she holds in Homer and Shakespeare's retellings, walks out on a job as a cocktail waitress in order to set up a hair braiding stand on the beach. This poem's Hector meets his death, not at the hands of a greater warrior, but with his hands on the wheel of the taxi he speeds back and forth on the winding mountain roads between the airport and the island's hotels (cf. Derek's thought that Hector died for Helen and for tourism, 230). The scramble for tourist money here claims lives as it sustains life. What ultimate impact do these invited invaders have on the poem, on the island? I'd like to focus on Walcott's ambiguous sense of national identity by analyzing a single image from his poem, namely, the picture postcard.

Walcott directs the reader's eye carefully in this poem, following the curve of a woman's back, the brushstrokes of a Winslow Homer masterpiece, the movements of crowds; at one point, to depict Hector's death, he even constructs a tragic cinematic montage, a la *The Battleship Potemkin*—cut to a leopard galloping, cut to a woman's hands, cut to the hubcap, cut to the face, etc. (230). Thus by invoking a postcard view of his poem, he demonstrates a narrowing of the already shallow human vision, one that demands a poet with the proper panoptic perspective.

Walcott notices early in the poem, in the voice of a white British expatriate from the comfort of a Range Rover, that St. Lucia's "past was flat as a postcard, and their future, / a brighter and flatter postcard, printed the schemes/ of charters with their poverty-guaranteed tour"

(57). Of course, while the reader must trust Plunkett's assessment of the island's bright, flat future, one must disagree with the flat vision of the past—I was going to say that there are various strata of pasts, but I'll instead use Walcott's Nobel lecture metaphor. Far from being flat, the island is a round vase recreated lovingly from shards of historical, cultural, religious, linguistic, national, and racial struggles. Thus, within the poem's first chapter, Walcott demonstrates the poetic task at hand, namely, to give these flat postcard people fullness, to make them breathe and live.

Even native St. Lucians are susceptible to such a view of the island, as is evident in Derek's walk through the town plaza, sepia'd in his mind as a postcard draining of color (69) until the light of a bluer postcard fills the sky (70). Now, this is a more accurate, loving image ... far from restricting the beauty of the island to a 4X6, Walcott is honest about the difficulty, the dimming of memory. This postcard vision, however, limits Derek's poetic craft when he leaves the island. While museum hopping in America, our narrator notices that, for tourists, every view becomes "a postcard signed by great names" (183)—Van Gogh's bench, Canaletto's sky. Watching a bird shoot through the slit window of an ancient Irish castle, Derek crafts the following less-than-Homeric simile: The bird flew through like a card dropped in a post-box. At least the photo-maniacal tourists of *Omeros*' opening episode are in a sort of active relationship with the island. Walcott and his characters may shout them down as clicking Cyclopes (299), but these visitors bring home a personalized representation—they cut out things, they emphasize others, they focus differently than a native might, they enter the experience in some cases. St. Lucia's danger, in contrast, is in allowing the world to be written, allowing the vision of their own lives to be crafted for them. The life being crafted for them/in spite of them threatens to push most St. Lucians out of the frame, as it were.

From the comfortable backseat of a taxi, Derek passes judgment on the "progress" of his home ... economic change pushing the coastal villages out of the way of asphalt roads, taming the wild savannah, paralyzing the peace "in a postcard, a concrete future" (227). In the last chapters of the poem, Walcott—without a shred of irony, without a sense of horror—quite simply calls it a postcard archipelago (290). What, then, endures besides the pretty pictures?

Well, Walcott's answer to the question "What endures?" is in some ways a false one.[1] The home that he celebrates fights a daily war of self-parody, and he might be guilty of, in his own words, "making a paradise of their poverty." The island is selling her soul; the island is movin' (cf. the beach DJ's cry at 112) but in no particular direction. Though he admires the spirit and community of the island's fishermen, this occupation is dwindling in its members and fading in its economic viability. So Walcott does what he can to see—and direct the reader's vision—outside the postcard's frame.

He protects many sections of his island from the awkward curiosity of its visitors. The beaches may be littered with (and by) so many tourists that it is difficult for the staff to serve them (see "Lawrence of St. Lucia," a waiter working the beach at 23), but the sea and the sky are largely free of them. Ocean liners and airplanes, certainly, bring tourists to the island, but Walcott and his characters rarely comment on, much less notice, such intrusions.[2] Moreover, the depth of the sea is plumbed only by St. Lucia's most heroic figure, Achille; the skies are measured only by St. Lucia's divine portents, by St. Lucia's earliest foreign visitors, the sea swifts. In addition, the mountain and the forest are regions traversed only with great difficulty and only by the most knowledgeable locals, not with the ease of a sun-baked visitor swinging his sandals from his finger. Finally, there are these very knowledgeable locals like Ma Kilman the healer and Seven Seas the blind seer, both far from the fashionable areas of the island, both participating in a sort of divine wisdom, but both old, childless . . . none will follow in their vocations, none will take up their paths. All readers, Walcott demonstrates, are mere tourists in the world of the epic—we can get a quick look at it, and we can even walk a while within it, outfitted in tacky foreign garb, speaking a different tongue in strident tones, returning to our comfortable homes and thanking God for our more fortunate fate. The only people, such as they are today, with entrance into the world of heroic struggle are the suffering, the isolated, the poor. Accordingly, then, Walcott provides for a telling final glimpse of the poem's surviving heroes, Achille and Philoctete.

One dawn while going to fish, Achille notices that due to the greed of fellow fishermen (who catch more than they need), he must row "farther out [from the island] / than he wanted to go" (300), so far out that "he felt betrayed / by his calling" (300). At sea the next morning, Philoctete is surprised to see the impossible, "the reefs were traveling / faster than they were" (302). What they thought was a reef turns out to be "*Baleine* [a whale]," an occupational hazard the likes of which Walcott never hints at in this epic hymn to the sea.[3] Far from being broken apart by the whale's tail, the ship—*In God We Troust*—is sprayed with a "bouquet of spume" then lifted above "the shelf of the open sea" and set back down (303). Walcott ends this baptism at/by the sea with the following wisdom:

> He has seen the shut face of thunder,
> he has known the frightening trough dividing the soul
>
> from this life and the other, he has seen the pod
> burst into spray. The bilge was bailed out, the sail
> turned home, their wet, salted faces shining with God. (303)

On the one hand, though he admires these fishermen—these "whom Jesus first drew to His net," these whose life "smelled strong and true" ("What the Twilight Says" 15)—their occupation is dwindling in its numbers and its economic viability;[4] on the other hand, this fate—at sea, together, smiling in the light of God—is better than any brochure can promise, truer than any postcard could show.

Notes

1. In this false comic resolution, Walcott's poem is perfectly Homeric. For all *Iliad* 24's tender solemnity between Achilleus and Priam, Achilleus must die, Troy must fall; the reunion of Ithaka's royal family is a similarly potent distraction from a more difficult poetic promise—Odysseus must leave Penelope.
2. In the most prominent scene featuring the path of an ocean liner, Walcott's Maud notices a liner while surveying her garden; Walcott crafts a delicately natural approach for this seacraft: "A liner grew . . . white as a lily, its pistil an orange stack" (122). Conversely, the "[s]low as a liner" approach of Helen, Maud's former housemaid, becomes violent, causing Maud to swear (cf. 123). In effect, Walcott demonstrates, outsiders do less damage to the islanders than the islanders themselves.
3. According to this poem, some readers might think that the sea offers no dangers save military ones (cf. the Battle of the Saints, chapters XIV-XV).
4. In the novel *Far Tortuga*, Peter Matthiessen's Caribbean fishermen also wonder whether they might not all be better off in the very near future carting tourists around, as Walcott's Hector does until his death, rather than "cotching" turtle (18).

Works Cited

Hirsch, Edward. "The Art of Poetry XXXVII: Derek Walcott." *Conversations with Derek Walcott*. Ed. William Baer. Jackson, Mississippi: UP of Mississippi, 1996.

Matthiessen, Peter. *Far Tortuga*. New York: Vintage Contemporaries, 1975.

Walcott, Derek. *Omeros*. New York: Noonday Press, 1990.

---. *Remembrance and Pantomime: Two Plays*. New York: Farrar, Straus, and Giroux, 1980.

---. "What the Twilight Says" (1970). *What the Twilight Says: Essays*. New York: Farrar, Straus, and Giroux, 1998.

Lyric and the Skill of Life

Eileen Gregory
University of Dallas

In these meditations on poems of Emily Dickinson, I hope to suggest briefly what a study of lyric poetry offers to students within a core curriculum. It offers something absolutely vital, especially in the context of other studies that train and discipline the mind, that teach the student "critical thinking." The study of the lyric teaches something quite other than critical thinking, and certainly something distinct from common or conventional notions of the interior life. In the context of a common culture that so brutalizes and trivializes the life of affection, desire, and reflection, lyric poetry offers a kind of counter-terrorism training of the heart and mind. Even in the context of the intellectual life pursued with integrity, the study of lyric poetry brings something invaluable to the student's experience, not contained in traditional notions of mastery.

I have long been bemused by a comment in a letter of Emily Dickinson to her favorite cousins: "Each of us gives or takes heaven in corporeal person, for each of us has the skill of life. It is not known of any bee that it failed of its flower, though known in specific instances through scarlet experience" (*Letters* 2.504). I can't entirely unpack this complex erotic metaphor of the flower destined for its bee—but what arrests me is the aphoristic claim, that "each of us" can negotiate her daily interchange with "heaven"—moments of erotic completion—

because each has "the skill of life." What is this skill? It is certainly more than an instinctual drive toward pleasure, because it is discretionary: a training, a discipline, that allows one openness and responsiveness to the amplitude of a specific encounter. This "skill of life" is deliberate and knowing—like the consciousness of the "fainting bee," in another poem, who, "Reaching late his flower, / Round her chamber hums, / Counts his nectars - enters, / And is lost in balms!" (211). The bee approaching his flower—as a metaphor for one entering "Eden"—defers pleasure ("Round her chamber hums") in order to take calculative measure of it beforehand ("Counts his nectars"), so that he *fully knows* at the moment that he is *wholly lost to knowing*. But this skill, while prudential and keen, is founded in a habit of risk-taking, rather than control—perhaps, in the life of the mind, the greatest risk of all, to stake everything upon the circuitous truth of metaphor. Dickinson takes metaphor not as illustration of thought or emotional state, but as an extravagant gesture of incarnation, the ground of all possible knowing and certainty.

I take this "skill of life" to be something that only poetry can impart: poetry that in its persistent reorientations and demands upon the reader disciplines and habituates both feeling and mind to moments of threshold apprehension and exchange.

My first reflection today suggests the kind of knowing that the discipline of lyric allows. So I am beginning, in a way, with suggesting the end, a shaped and oriented attention to the world and to the other. The second meditation asks how, through Dickinson's poetry, one is trained or enabled to see this way.

I
Her Grace is all she has—
And that, so least displays—
One Art to recognize, must be,
Another Art, to praise—(J810)

This epigram points to (and enacts) a distinctive mode of apprehension and speech, oriented to the task of seeing grace and saving it. It is of course the task of this poet, who has trained her eye to discern the barely manifest and trained her speech to render its significance. But this mode also belongs to the reader—and the critic— asked to catch the bare grace of the epigram itself, its economy and sharpness, and find fitting language to acknowledge it. And of course, its grace is all that *any* poem possesses: it *is* its grace, or it is nothing if it is without its grace.

The epigram certainly points to some of the principles of Dickinson's own poetic economy, but, more generally, it also points to a kind of knowing and a kind of ethical response that lyric poetry especially cultivates. The poem names certain "Arts" necessitated by the hidden, diminutive nature of this grace. I would like for a moment to take seriously this sense that the discernment and preservation of "grace" within the world entails art: that is to say, a deliberately cultivated skill, an habitual focus of both mind and affection, a discipline of attention. The arts enacted by the poet are open to the reader willing to accept their difficult conditions. The steady and serious reader Dickinson hopes for comes to share in the economy of grace—the ascetics of perception, feeling, and thought—that grounds her discipline.

This poem illumines the bases of this economy. The quality at the heart of the poem—her Grace—is never defined. It is not that the poet assumes from the outset a common meaning of "grace," but quite the opposite. This Grace does not belong to the common arena. It is at the periphery, failing to manifest itself in clear social markers. Certainly it is not glamour, or beauty in any obvious sense—"features" or "accomplishments"—since these things carry a sense of deliberate display, opulence, or spectacle. Dickinson asks the reader from the beginning to participate in a circulation of goods outside the marketplace. Along with the marginality of Grace is its condition of impoverishment. This Grace is twice constituted within poverty—"all she has" implying "*nothing* else," "so least displays" implying "*nothing* more." Poverty is of course a constant in Dickinson's poetry. But if we take her seriously, this "theme" arises not so much from personal disposition—from whatever sources in her biography or religious beliefs—as from the necessities compelling her poetic economy. Marginality, poverty, and diminution belong to this territory.

The hidden quality of this Grace, then, requires the "Art to recognize": the ability to see something rare and crucial outside of conventional codes. It is a knowing conditioned by lack, and therefore attentive to peripheral, barely discernible disclosures. How—by what signs—has her Grace been disclosed to the poet? We are not told; and, in the denial of explanation, we can only guess. But in fact this guessing constitutes the reader's own performance of "recognition"— for we are asked to confirm our common experience of this *kind* of fragile epiphany within ordinary life—"re-cognition" because her grace is something already known, though perhaps not acknowledged. Her grace resides, one guesses, in the merest shadow of a gesture, but a gesture that implies her whole bearing in the world, her distinct, habitual accommodation to life. It is as though a gesture were in the mind's eye an arc, projecting a contour, a visage. Whatever the signs of her grace, grasped by the poet, guessed by the reader, they suggest not something accidental or occasional about her, but an intrinsic quality, a disposition carried in the least thing, perhaps *only* in the least thing.

Clearly it is an "art" to recognize this grace—because it is difficult to see, because it necessitates an almost ascetic habit of perception. It is another difficult "Art to praise." Why? Because it goes against the grain to praise something so little and obscure. Praise belongs to the public arena, which is grounded upon another, opposite economy of value. This act of praise must do justice to the fragile but crucial life, manifest so marginally, and it must therefore, itself, participate in its hiddenness and austerity.

Whatever the difficulty of these "Arts," this poem insists that recognizing and praising are not only appropriate but necessary to the poetic economy. Recognition entails not abstract and detached perception, but participatory and evaluative judgment—acknowledgment of human commonality. And praise here does not confirm values within conventional discourse. It is, rather, a gesture of celebration that points to being. Praise is a mode of ontological speech, giving the indiscernible and the hidden a discrete, discriminated being in human terms. It is—further—a gesture of gratitude, possessing the open-ended quality of thankfulness for gifts bestowed. In this sense, it is crucial to the alternate economy of exchange that the poem points to—a circulation of goods outside of public commodities, oriented toward giving and receiving grace within mortal contingencies.

So I am suggesting that if indeed the lyric trains one in seeing grace and saving it, that discipline is rooted in awareness of all those human things least acknowledged or valued in common currency—even in the common currency of intellectual life—because we teach our students intellectual mastery, control, articulateness, fluency, all those things that can allow them a place in the world, that can overcome their natural experience of poverty, destitution, marginality, insufficiency. We want them to be rich, not poor, as indeed we wish ourselves to be rich. We as teachers are perhaps in an unacknowledged conspiracy with them, not to confirm our own destitution, or theirs, in the midst of our privileged enterprise. However, that feeling of disorientation and loss is always, for young people and perhaps for their teachers, right below the surface. Poetry gives a place for it; it discriminates and names it; it allows for grief and consolation; it reveals its powers to them, its benefits of integrity and largesse.

The lyric, to be most blunt, is valuable to education because it opens our students, in the most reflective and complex way, to the experience of exposure and lack, out of which, alone, the experience of joy and sufficiency is possible. This is not a new idea: Plato's Diotima tells the story that the mother of Eros is Penia, want, Poverty, while his father is Plenty (*Symposium* 203b-204b*)*. The very ground of desire, which for Plato, for Dante, is the basis of all knowledge, resides in this experience of mortal poverty. This principle is central to Dickinson's poetry—her constant reiteration that longing; the longing that takes one farthest in hope of happiness comes out of poverty and not plenty. In the words of one of her late poems, Want is "a quiet Commissary / For Infinity" (J1036). We know best what we do not possess, not what we possess. Plenty opens itself to view at certain moments, then withdraws, leaving a greater desire that compels attendance upon, waiting for, another moment of brief possession. Plenty and Poverty constitute the axis mundi of the lyric universe, in the context of which it engages us in a habit of reflection grounded in mortal contingency, opposing common norms of avoidance and easy consolation. This experience of hunger and thirst in the face of a revealed but denied happiness can often be tragic and devastating, but, for Dickinson, the brilliant light of loss alone reveals the extent and power of human spirit. That experience of loss, strangely, is the ground as well for joy.

One of Dickinson's best-known poems points to this economy founded in the impoverishment of desire.

Success is counted sweetest
By those who ne'er succeed.
To comprehend a nectar
Requires sorest need.

Not one of all the purple Host
Who took the Flag today
Can tell the definition
So clear of Victory

As he defeated —dying—
On whose forbidden ear

> The distant strains of triumph
> Burst agonized and clear! (J67)

Here, as in so many other of Dickinson's poems, a deeply emotional suffering is a cognitive apprehension. There is no separation in her sensibility between feeling and knowing. The poem emphasizes the clarity and brilliance of an act of knowing, coming with the experience of utter destitution—success is "counted" sweetest to one denied success; one "comprehends" a nectar only in need; one "tell[s] the definition" of victory only in defeat. Dickinson is claiming here that—in lyric terms—the basis of knowing is in the acute apprehension opened through loss.

However, another poem suggests a different aspect of this paradox—a revelation of presence, withdrawn, that leaves behind a longing necessitating the reordering of one's desire.

> In many and reportless places
> We feel a Joy—
> Reportless, also, but sincere as Nature
> Or Deity—
>
> It comes, without a consternation—
> Dissolves—the same—
> But leave a sumptuous Destitution—
> Without a Name—
>
> Profane it by a search—we cannot
> It has no home—
> Nor we who having once inhaled it—
> Thereafter roam. (J1382)

Lyric poetry speaks essentially about events that are "reportless"—this strangely repeated word in the poem—marginal, outside of the public account, below or beyond fact; it speaks of a grace that is untranslatable and uncodifiable. The ephemeral event of joy, the poem implies, constitutes the spiritual substance of corporeal life—"sincere [pure, whole, true or real] as Nature / Or Diety." However full, it does not satisfy or satiate desire, but rather magnifies Want, giving it amplitude and richness—leaving behind "a sumptuous Destitution / Without a Name." This is a palpable longing that cannot be located or fixed—an orientation to the invisible, the "infinite," the unknown and unknowable. The poem—in its via negativa—describes the attributes of grace—unaccountable, placeless, nameless, unclaimable—that empties one by its fullness.

Whether in its manifestation as tragic devastation or as sumptuousness, the experience of poverty constitutes human identity, opening the landscape of the interior life. Out of poverty comes longing, and human knowing and loving have amplitude only to the degree that longing is acknowledged and cultivated. "Longing, it may be, is the gift no other gift supplies" (Dickinson, *Letters* 2.499).

Robert Duncan in an early segment of the "H.D. Book" arrives at the comment that he values in H.D.'s poetry precisely those things that, he says, "rescue it from what is correct and invulnerable" (10). I am struck by this reversal of terms—the idea of risk that rescues poetry from the invulnerable. The invulnerable signifies those attitudes that give one the illusion of stability, certainty, and control: the appeal to conceptual mastery, institutional consensus, monumentality. More broadly, it is indeed a function of lyric to rescue language, to rescue human things, to rescue the reader, from the invulnerable.

If lyric has a place within a core curriculum, it is precisely to perform this rescue, which is all the more necessary when a curriculum consists of canonical, "classic" texts, which all too easily come to seem in service to invulnerable structures. The lyric performs continually a sense of the risk and danger of reading. The challenge in teaching lyric is to make its dangerousness felt, to allow its edge to cut. At the heart of learning, one might say, is the capability of always acknowledging that condition of dereliction out of which alone we can know the preciousness of what we love. The lyric puts us in this danger: that is its irreplaceable value within education.

Notes

1. The implications of Dickinson's diction—for instance, *sincere, sumptuous, destitution*—are clarified with reference to Noah Webster's *An American Dictionary of the English Language* (1828), <http://www.cbtministries.org/resources/webster1828.htm>. The 1844 edition of this dictionary was Dickinson's beloved Lexicon.

Works Cited

Dickinson, Emily. *The Complete Poems of Emily Dickinson*, ed. Thomas H. Johnson. Boston: Little Brown, 1960.

---. *The Letters of Emily Dickinson.* Johnson, Thomas H., ed. Cambridge: Belknap Press of Harvard University, 1958.

Duncan, Robert. "Beginnings. Chapter 1 of the H.D. Book. Part I" *Coyote's Journal* 5-6 (1966): 8-31.

Plato. *Symposium.* 203b-204b.

Achieving (Comm)Unity in Difference Through the Core Text

D.W. Hadley
University of Dallas

Three integrations—three instances of achieving community—are made possible by the use of core texts in the genuinely liberal classroom. First is an integration cultivated in the individual student, the nurturing of each particular human being, who is shaped by the reading, writing, thinking, speaking (etc.) tasks imposed during a semester, towards a genuine community, wherein each part serves the whole knowingly and willingly. Second is an integration achieved in the classroom and its immediate surroundings—the college campus (or a portion thereof)—whereby the students come to know each other and to know how to communicate with each other through the tasks demanded by a liberal arts course. Third is an integration—a development of genuine unity among different individuals and groups of individuals—found outside (or *after*) college life: what the individual student and groups of students learn to do inside and outside of the college classroom (and its surroundings) enables the formation of healthy community in the social involvements that will be undertaken by students after their graduation.

All three of these communities are achieved through the interplay of self- and other-discovery that takes place through (in fact, is demanded by) close, careful, open readings of such core texts as Sigmund Freud's *The Future of an Illusion*, Descartes' *Meditations*, and Plato's

Republic. Let us begin with the first integration, that is, the building up of the community that is in—rather, that is—the individual student, with reference to the two courses that I taught at the University of Dallas (UD) in the Fall of 2004, both core philosophy courses. The first course was our introductory human nature class, titled "Philosophy of Man" and required of all students at UD. The second was an elective course that fulfills the fourth philosophy course requirement and is taken by every education major and a number of other students: Philosophy of Education. How did our work with core texts in these courses build up individual community; that is, bring to life and order an internal integration of powers and capacities in each particular student? Generally speaking, each awakened the student to the riches of their own inner depths. The texts alerted them to their own ontological make-up, drawing explicit attention to parts of themselves not seen or only fuzzily attended to previously, thereby allowing them to come into greater possession and make fuller use of themselves. More particularly, Freud's *The Future of an Illusion*, introduced with ample background, drew the attention of the students to their inner basement, to the cluster of hidden psychological drives or motivations, whether spawned in childhood experiences, or built in to the structure of their being, or some of both. More qualified, I might say that Freud drew their attention to the possibility of hidden urges and desires, lusts and loathings, aspirations and apprehensions, moving them from inside. For by no means did each student receive in the same way such remarks by Freud as "every individual is virtually an enemy of civilization" (6) and "[t]here are countless civilized people who would shrink from murder or incest but who do not deny themselves the satisfaction of their aggressive urges or their sexual lusts, and who do not hesitate to injure other people by lies, fraud and calumny, so long as they can remain unpunished for it . . ." (14; cf. 18). The range of reactions to Freud's vision of Man as instinct-driven animal was varied. Yet I added force to the Freudian thesis by applying examples from Freud's other writings, wherein, with charm and, I believe, insight, he illustrates how much of our individual thinking and acting are driven by unseen "psychological" influences. Students often laughed at themselves, I think, in laughing at the slips of tongue and behavioral neuroses (etc.) of Freud's patients.

In respect to the two other texts I mentioned above, Descartes' *Meditations* and Plato's *Republic*, similar insights were made, similar self-discoveries approached, when I demanded that students ask and answer for themselves how one can be sure of anything inside or outside of oneself once one adopts Descartes' method of radical doubt (see *Meditations* I), also by asking them to consider what in their own personal experience could be used to justify the Platonic claim (from *Republic* IX) that there is a terrible thing, a lawless beast of some kind, inside us.

So far, then, I have tried to show that something simple but profound has been happening in my courses in respect to community-building. Students have come face to face with themselves as complex wholes requiring attention, understanding, ordering, through close contact with core texts, texts that have a number of core concerns held curiously in common, texts that all alike (though differently) speak to our human core.

Now let us turn to the second instance of community-building. On this count, which builds upon the first count, community becomes (more) possible through the cultivated classroom interaction of ever more complex student-individual with ever more complex student-individual. On this count, students who are coming into greater familiarity with themselves are asked to come into greater familiarity with each other. On this count, the classroom is presented as a place of encounter, which is not an exception but a rule. "We are here to talk with each other, to learn from each other," I repeat (*ad nauseam*, I fear). Our interaction is guided by our core texts. The core texts create common space in which to learn how to be a classroom community through creating space in which individual opinions and personalities are allowed to come forth and express themselves—together, in which mutual understanding is achieved through the open declaration of this or that individual coming into contact with the declarations of others. Please note just how important the core text is for such coming together. Among other things, it gives us a source for weighty issues to be discussed as relevant to all, though open to much difference of opinion. For instance, one does not shy away from the claim that Descartes is right, that he gives us "at least a point that we can't fall past," as several students have put their take on the *cogito*. Indeed, one rightly puts this interpretation "out there" for consideration, with strong encouragement for students to consider their own experience through Cartesian lenses, thereby paving the road for a classroom coming together. That is, one makes direct, explicit use of student comments in cultivating discussion. For another instance, how awkward things become when I ask the students to tell me if they would ever make use of Descartes' first argument on behalf of God's existence (stated thus by Descartes: "I have no choice but to conclude that the mere fact of my existing and of there being in me an idea of a most perfect being, that is, God, demonstrates most evidently that God too exists" [80]): will you use this in your own conversations and thinking about God?' In the most recent situation, initial responses were relatively noncommittal and innocuous, but once one student declared that you cannot convince anybody of God's existence if they don't already in some way believe, we were off to the races. For once, that student touched a nerve (of students for whom reason is a God-given guide in wending one's way through the darkness of a fallen world back up to the divine light); genuine encounter of real opinion with real opinion took place. Similar real-life encounters of student with student, with consequent lessons in getting along with different viewpoints (i.e., building of community), were cultivated through discussion of Freud's and Plato's texts. And I should point out that I consciously cultivated such encounters: I ask the students to say what they really think; I warn them that disagreements will occur; I encourage them to seek to work through the disagreements, if only to understand better how someone reading the same text would react to it so differently. Let me also highlight the fact that in my view, if one does not advise students openly of the fittingness (and benefits) of such encounters, they might be content to state a personal opinion and just leave it at that—leave the misguided others to their foolishness, if you will. Rather, I suggest that we should grapple with the text together; grapple with the text and with each other more thoroughly than with simply ourselves to seek a common understanding and good through our ever more common study of the text.

It is from this experience of community-building in and through classroom encounters with core texts that I derive the title of my talk: I am continually humbled by those moments of learning to talk with— for extended periods of time, on matters of tremendous difficulty and importance—people with whom one disagrees, perhaps strongly. My claim is this: to learn how to talk with those with whom you disagree, even vehemently, is to build (even achieve) community. As a matter of fact, I consider this kind of community to be the one most desirable in the world today. If we can do it in the classroom, we can do it more largely, with the help of texts big enough to interest, challenge, inform, discipline, and order all. It is intriguing to observe how what happens inside the classroom on this count spills over into campus life more largely.

And this leads to my third point, for which I have little time or space left. This seems fitting, however, because my third and final claim is actually terribly speculative. Here it is: the college classroom that forces the student to engage in common endeavors to understand a text that is called core—called such because it presumes to speak to our core in some significant way, and teaches us about it even through the effort to understand its still hidden insights (that is, a core text educates along the way, not simply at the end of the journey)—builds a community above and beyond the classroom and the classroom's immediate environs (i.e., the campus). Its bringing into unity of diverse students (even at places, like UD, which at first glance appear to be monolithic unities of the most conventional sort) plants a community ideal in them; it builds their community muscles, if you will. When they encounter different opinions outside the classroom, they are not surprised; when they hear something they do not understand or agree with, they know how to express their confusion or disagreement. They know how to lean in, not dismiss, instinctively; they look for common ground, perhaps even a common good (which is one mark of the core text as such); they already know what it is like to work through to an understanding. Indeed, they will look for the text that is being interpreted, rightly or wrongly, by their discussion partner, even if it is the hard-to-grasp text of that person's own experience or cultural context. For this they have been prepared, especially by a text such as Plato's *Republic*, which has these encounters at its forefront, a text that is utilized so very well at the University of Dallas, with precisely this commonweal venture in mind. After all, it is the core text itself (there may be no better example than the *Republic*) that warns the reader that private discussions (if you will, classroom discussions) are not an end in themselves. They stem from something larger. They are incomplete until funneling into, contributing to, something larger. In Platonic terms, this "something larger" is the polis, for Glaucon is called by name at the end of the dialogue (see *Republic* 621C) to lend himself to his community and its greatest good, having already seen himself in light of the whole that is the cosmic community and its divine good. "Are you ready?" Socrates seems to be asking. "Have you learned?" he declares in a not so uncertain whisper. So it is in the course that treats this core text with the respect it so richly deserves. Our discussion of it—our discussion itself—is just the beginning. A larger discussion, with much higher stakes, awaits, as a larger life and world than the classroom and campus await, as well. It is that community which I believe to be built-up by the work done in a college classroom dedicated to giving core texts (should I say genuine core texts?), and their students, their fullest due.

My concluding remarks take the shape of reminders and caveats, of which I have several. First is that I wish to point out that my view of good community described above is not my view of the highest community. People who are profoundly different having fruitful conversations with each other and not being annoyed or violent—yes, this is indeed good community; but there is a community that lies beyond such agreeableness-in-difference which I believe to be the highest form of community available to humankind, one where similarity (at least on some fundamental matters) is the dominant note. But in our diverse, difficult, democratic modern world, the penultimate good community is a worthy enough goal to strive for. Second, I do not think that the above given instances of integration-building can occur best without the teacher drawing attention to them for their sake and for the sake of the students. That is, community-building such as I have described must be consciously cultivated; a great part of their coming true relies on the professor telling the students that "this is what we are up to." Third, what this goal entails is some very significant emphasis and reliance upon discussion in the classroom: the classroom must be student and discussion centered, or else this means of community-building will fail. And as part of this student and discussion emphasis, I should note that the cultivation of difference—surprises, challenges, disagreements, discomfort—is terribly important. I am committed to the view that the (typical) student will (typically) grow most through the unpleasant encounter with somebody who sees things differently and might actually be right—or, more right (especially through learning the lesson that one is not always right). That this can take place through the student's individual encounter with the text itself is of course a desirable possibility. Finally, please note how speculative I have been in regard to the third community. I have not polled my graduates on this count, apart from casual conversations that take place here and there, nor am I aware of any such study. I do not withdraw my claim, as it stands to reason to make it, yet it remains speculative.

Works Cited
Descartes, Rene. *Meditations on First Philosophy*. Trans. Donald A. Cress. 4th ed. Indianapolis, IN: Hackett, 1998.

Freud, Sigmund. *The Future of an Illusion*. Ed. James Strachey. Trans. W.D. Robson-Scott. NY/London: W.W. Norton and Co., 1961 [1989].

Plato. *Republic*. Trans. G.M.A. Grube. Indianapolis: Hackett, 1992.

Literary Experiences of Community

The Music of Democracy
Core Values in Core Texts

Paul Woodruff
University of Texas at Austin

Cleocritus has a beautiful voice. We must believe this, because he is the announcer at the religious initiations at Eleusis—where all Athenians—men, women, foreign residents, and even some slaves—may go to be born again, out of darkness and into the light, in order that they could expect to have special protection from the gods in the life to come.

Cleocritus has a beautiful voice, and now he has an opportunity to use it for a good cause in *this* world: peace, and harmony. The year is 403 Before the Common Era, and Athens has recently lost its long war with Sparta. A group of thirty has been installed in power by the victorious Spartans, and they have established an aristocratic government for Athens, a government in which only three thousand men, chosen by the thirty, have voting and legal rights. Fearing an uprising against them, these thirty men have conducted a reign of terror against supporters of democracy, so that Athens is now embroiled in civil war. This action earns them the name by which they are known to history—as the Thirty Tyrants—"tyrants" being the word for rulers who rule by violently instilling fear in their subjects, out of the fear that their subjects might violently displace them.

In order to understand what is at stake, you need to know this about Athenian democracy: the right to vote, the right to bring lawsuits, the right to make proposals in the Assembly, and the obligation to serve in official positions—all these belonged to every male citizen, and the majority of citizens were poor wage earners who were not landowners. Knowing that elections generally favored the rich, Athens filled most official positions by a lottery that treated all citizens equally, and the two representative bodies (the council and the lawmakers) were also filled by lottery.[1]

The rich and wellborn feared the power of the poor; that is why they agitated against democracy, and why their agitation sometimes flamed into civil war. What was democratic about this system was that it gave genuine power to the poor, treating them equally with the rich. It was not perfect democracy—that has not occurred anywhere—but its defects were those of all political systems in its time and place. It did not give equal power to women, to foreign residents, or to slaves. It was therefore not fully democratic in our modern sense, but it was democratic enough to terrify the rich.

Once the Thirty initiated their reign of terror, the democrats started fleeing the city one by one, gathering in an outpost named Phylê. There they formed an army and fended off an attack by the Thirty. Soon after, they crept into the Piraeus—the port of Athens—where they enjoyed almost unanimous support from the people, and where citizens flocked to them in increasing numbers. Then the Thirty came down to the Piraeus with their army, but finding the democrats in control of the high ground (both literally and morally) the army of the Thirty was roundly defeated.

After the battle, both sides agreed to a truce during which they could collect their dead. And it was during this truce that Cleocritus found his voice and spoke to the aristocratic army. This was the army that had driven his people out of their own city, and, although they had been defeated, they were still in control of the city of Athens. This speech is given us by the historian Xenophon, who continues Thucydides' tradition of reporting speeches as he thinks they ought to have been given:

> Citizens, why are you keeping us out of Athens? Why do you want to kill us? We never did anything bad to you. Not at all. We have joined with you in the holiest rituals, in the most beautiful sacrifices and festivals. We have been fellow dancers with you, fellow students, and fellow soldiers. We have undergone many dangers with you on land and sea for the sake of our common freedom and safety. For gods' sake—for the sake of the gods of our fathers and mothers—for the sake of our kinship, our marriage ties, and our fellowship—because many of us share in all these—show reverence to gods and men. Put a stop to this crime against our city, and cease to obey those Thirty, those horribly irreverent men, who, in eight months, have killed almost more Athenians than the Peloponnesians did in ten years of war. (Xenophon, qtd. in Woodruff, *First Democracy* 83)

Cleocritus' beautiful voice has an effect. The surviving leaders of the Thirty do not want their troops listening to such talk. They lead the defeated army back to Athens. Next day, for the first time, the friends and supporters of the Thirty had turned against them. The three thousand citizens, the ones to whom the Thirty had given voting rights, vote them out of office. And the Thirty, who have driven so many good Athenians into exile, must now leave the city for a place of safety.

The Thirty, and the Three Thousand, are still relying on the Spartans to save them. But now Sparta no longer sees an advantage in supporting this unpopular regime. Sparta does not want to abandon its friends in Athens entirely, however, and so the Spartan leadership asks the Athenians on both sides to swear an oath of reconciliation and amnesty. Only the Thirty and a few others are to be punished. After that, there will be peace.

The oath of reconciliation and amnesty did bring peace into Athens, and a fair degree of harmony. The oath held. On both sides, the swearing must have been heartfelt, and not merely mouthed to please the Spartans. Cleocritus had sounded what Abraham Lincoln, at the outset of the American Civil War, would call "the mystic chords of memory."[2] These chords were strong in Athens, because Athenian men really did dance together at religious festivals. They really had a common education and military training. And they shared, along with their own memories of victory and defeat, myths of glory. In the festivals and theaters of Athens, singing and dancing together, they had shared the music of democracy.

Harmony was the most important of the core values of ancient democracy. Athens learned it the hard way after a century of intermittent class warfare. Their system, which began in 508 BCE and had fully evolved by about 461, had many flaws. But after 403, Athenian democracy improved: ostracism was eliminated, the power of the majority was curtailed, and attacks by the people against aristocrats came to an end.[3]

I learned about harmony the easy way—simply by thinking what "democracy" means.[4] If it means "government by the people" it entails a measure of harmony. It's not democracy if a majority rules tyrannically. That would not be government by the people, but government by PART of the people. Such government easily turns into the tyranny of the majority, if the majority is not held back and harnessed by law to work for the common good. And *tyranny* is contrary to democracy.[5]

The very notion of the common good depends on harmony. If the people are harshly divided, the common good will be elusive, and it will appear that whatever is good for one faction is thoroughly bad for another. In such a context, democracy will be impossible. In the first hundred years of democracy in Athens, class conflict was the bane of the system, always threatening to break out into civil war. From this the Athenians learned after 403 to set class conflict aside. A strength of our democracy now is the harmony that lies behind recent tax cuts in the United States: harmony is evident when poor people vote for tax cuts that benefit only the rich directly. If the poor were to use their power to make off with the wealth of the rich, that would begin to look like class warfare. Madison and other framers of the Constitution were opposed to democracy because they could not imagine this result; they insisted on limiting the vote to those with property, in order to protect the rich from the depredations they expected from the poor, if they allowed the poor to vote. Luckily for us, Madison was wrong, and our harmony has enabled us to maintain democracy without major class conflict since the vote was finally given to the poor. Athens, after 403, was in much the same condition. Taxes were much heavier on the rich than on the poor, but this seems to have been accepted by all sides, as an instance of proportional justice.

1. The First Chord: Harmony

So harmony is a core value of democracy. It is celebrated in many core texts of the Greek classics, and it was expressed in the ceremonial culture of the Athenians, which brought citizens together through music, dance, theater, and religious processions. But harmony is easily misunderstood. *Political* harmony is as difficult to grasp as the art of politics itself.

The Greek word is *homonoia*—"like-mindedness." For this the ancient Greeks used a number of images. Plato thought that in order to achieve political harmony you must train all citizens "to sing one song" (*Republic* 432a). Luckily, most Greek thinkers did not agree. The essence of political harmony is accepting differences within a structure that allows all citizens to work together for certain common goals—such as defense, religion, and education. About religion, keep in mind that polytheism—the worship of many gods—intrinsically allows a wide range of diversity. About education I have a lot to say, later.

First, a look at two famous non-musical images for harmony. The first is Aesop's famous bundle of sticks:

> A farmers' sons used to quarrel, and though he tried many times, he could not persuade them to change by means of arguments [*logoi*]; so he realized that he would have to do this through action, and he asked them to bring him a bundle of sticks. When they had done as they were told, he first gave them the sticks all together and ordered them to break the bundle. When they could not do this, no matter how much force they used, he then untied the bundle and gave sticks to them one at a time. These they broke easily, and he said, "So it is with you, my sons. If you are in harmony, you will be unconquerable by your enemies; but if you quarrel, you will be easily taken." (Gagarin and Woodruff 149)

This fable, attributed to Aesop, comes from the time when democracy was evolving in Greece. The ancient moralist who collected the fables added this moral: "The story shows that harmony is as strong as quarreling is easy to overcome." The language of the fable and its moral is political. For "quarreling" the Greek uses *stasis,* a word with meanings ranging from division into political factions all the way to outright civil war.

This story sounds good to many people, but it is a terrible model for politics. Consider:

a. It is about defense, about war, as if war is the only reason we have to work together. Peace is a far better reason to seek harmony.

b. It consists in absolute rigidity, and rigidity can be disastrous. If the only way to budge the bundle of sticks is to break or untie it, we should expect that eventually the power of circumstance will accomplish one of those:

You've seen trees tossed by a torrent in a flash flood:
If they bend, they're saved, and every twig survives,
But if they stiffen up they're washed out by the roots.
(Sophocles, *Antigone,* lines 712-14)

c. The harmony comes from outside: STRING or ROPE holds the sticks together, just as an unwilling army may be held together by a general, or a quarreling family by a patriarch. Subtract the general or the patriarch, and what looks like harmony shows its true colors. So the former Yugoslavia, when Tito died, came apart.

d. And the sticks all run the same way. In no real polity will citizens be content to lie parallel—they will not agree about their orientation—and they will not even pretend to do so unless they have been compelled by violence.

This is monstrous as a concept of political harmony.

My second image is more attractive, and more feminine. It has none of the faults of the bundle: Let the sticks go crosswise, weave them into a mat of some kind, and then they hold themselves together. Then the result is flexible. Weaving in the ancient world was women's work, and so the image of weaving belongs to women. The comic playwright Aristophanes imagines a scene in which women take over government, and this is their plan:

> Start out as you would with wool from a shearing:
> Put it in a tub and scrub the gobs of sheep shit off the city.
> Then spread it out and flog it to get rid of the bad guys—
> The sticker-burrs and those that organize themselves
> Into a tangle to get elected. Comb them out
> And pluck off their heads. After that, comb
> Good common will into a basket, mixing everyone
> Together. Resident aliens, foreigners (if you like them),
> And anyone who owes the city money—mix them all in.
> And for god's sake—these cities that are colonies of ours—
> Understand them as separate balls of wool, off
> By themselves. Take all of these and bring them together
> And join them into one, then spin them onto a huge
> Bobbin and weave from that a cloak for the people.
> — Lysistrata, in Aristophanes' *Lysistrata (574-86)* [6]

This comes from comedy, and the voice is a woman's. Women were not to be heard in public on any subject at this time in Athens, but even so, the ideas behind this image demand to be taken seriously. They are ideas that Aristophanes' audience wanted to entertain.

The most exciting idea is "weaving everyone together." Lysistrata believes in excluding only the people who do not have Athens' best interests at heart. Everyone else, citizens and non-citizens, even people from Athenian colonies, will be woven into the fabric of the state.

The weaving image is lovely, but it has a defect: the fabric is made of threads running in only two directions—the warp and the woof—a limitation Plato exploits in his use of the image in his dialogue entitled the *Statesmen*. There the goal is anti-democratic, and only two classes are woven together—soldiers and philosophers.

So I prefer the musical image—which also has a place in the Greek classics—and is especially fitting because the basis of harmony in Athens was music—the harmonious combination of poetry and rhythm and dance and melody, and, beyond that, the weaving of ideas across one another in dialogue. And all this harmony could be heard on the dramatic stage of Dionysus in Athens.

The music of democracy was sung in the tragic theater, and this was the greater part of public education under the democracy. Probably all male citizens danced in the choruses at one time in their lives, and many attended each year's plays. Attendance was so important that public money was used—the theoric fund—to encourage it.

2. The Second Chord: Equality

Political equality as an ideal is a major theme in ancient Greek tragedy. In Sophocles' *Antigone*, it shows up in several places—in the scene in which the lowly watchman runs rings around the tyrant in an interchange, and in the passage in which the tyrant's son insists that his father pay attention to the opinion of common people:

Creon
So you don't think this girl has been infected with crime?
Haemon
No. The people of Thebes deny it, all of them.
Creon
So you think the people should tell me what orders to give?
Haemon
Now who's talking like he's wet behind the ears?
Creon
So I should rule this country for someone other than myself?
Haemon
A place for one man alone is not a city.
Creon
A city belongs to its master. Isn't that the rule?
Haemon
Then go be ruler of a desert, all alone. You'd do it well. (712-14).[7]

More explicit statements of equality come from two fragments (surviving quotations from lost plays):

One day showed us all to be one tribe of humans,

Born from a father and a mother;
No one is by birth superior to another.
But fate nourishes some of us with misery
And some with prosperity, while others are compelled
To bear the yoke of slavery.
(Sophocles, qtd. in Gagarin and Woodruff 56, 24)

What a waste of words it is to speak
In praise of high birth for human beings!
Long ago, when we first came to be,
The earth that gave birth to mortals decided
To rear us all to have the same appearance.
We are nothing special:
The well-born and ill-born are one race,
But time and custom [*nomos*] brought about this haughtiness.
Intelligence may come by birth,
But good sense is a gift of the god, not wealth.
(Euripides, qtd. in Gagarin and Woodruff 70, 17) [8]

Needless to say, the Athenians were no more consistent in their application of this doctrine than were the signers of the Declaration of Independence, many of whom held slaves, most of whom had no intention of giving political equality to the poor, and none of whom imagined equal political rights for women. Still, both groups meant something by their words, something larger than they could fully grasp at the time they uttered them. The survival of the core idea of equality—in both ancient and modern texts—has been a crucial support in the ongoing battle to make political equality a reality.

3. The Third Chord: Freedom

Greek tragedy celebrates freedom primarily by holding up its privation to public view, bringing out its faults for all to see. The privation of freedom is tyranny, and the mark of tyranny in this scheme of things is hubris. Tyrants try to hold onto power by frightening their subjects, and they are moved to do so by their own fear of their subjects—that they, the tyrants, will be violently overthrown. And so they rule by violence, putting themselves above the law. Many of the tragic plays illustrate such behavior and show its devastating consequences. One play makes the point explicit, both the positive point about freedom and the negative one about tyranny:

> When the laws are written down, then he who is weak
> And he who is rich have equal justice . . .
> And a lesser man can overcome a greater one,
> If he has justice on his side.
> This is freedom: To ask, "Who has a good proposal
> He wishes to introduce for public discussion?"
> And one who responds gains fame, while one who wishes
> Not to is silent. What could be fairer than that in a city?
> And besides, when the people govern a country,
> They rejoice in the young citizens who are rising to power,
> Whereas a man who is king thinks them his enemy
> And kills the best of them and any he finds
> To be intelligent, because he fears for his power.
> How then could a city continue to be strong
> When someone plucks off the young men
> As if he were harvesting grain in a spring meadow?
> Why should one acquire wealth and livelihood
> For his children, if the struggle is only to enrich the tyrant further?
> Why keep his young daughters virtuously at home,
> To be the sweet delights of tyrants? . . .
> I'd rather die than have my daughters wed by violence.
> (Euripides, *Suppliant Maidens* 433-455, qtd. in Gagarin and Woodruff 00)

And one play sounds a theme known to us also from the philosophers, especially Plato, that being a tyrant is a personal disaster for the tyrant himself:

> Do you think anyone
> Would choose to rule in constant fear
> When he could sleep without trembling,
> And have exactly the same power? Not me.
> Why should I want to be Tyrant?

I'd be insane . . .(*Oedipus Tyrannus* 584-589, qtd. in Meineck and Woodruff)[9]

In this way, the poets of democracy grew a concept of freedom by contrast with what was, to them, its opposite. Freedom was a point of immense pride with the Athenians, and continued to inspire them to dreams of independence long after their city had been lost to the big armies of Macedon and Rome.

4. The Final Chords: Reverence and Justice

Many ancient thinkers held that justice and/or reverence are essential for the survival of any community. Plato built his argument in the Republic on the hypothesis that whatever is most important to the stability of a state will turn out to be justice. Reverence had a lesser place in his system, but earlier writers, especially poets, had treated reverence as equal to justice in importance.[10]

Although celebrated in every political system in antiquity, justice and reverence have a special value in democracy. Democracy depends on restraining all leaders under the rule of law, and law, to the ancients, was inextricable from justice. The tendency to think of law in positive terms—as simply constituted by political authority, right or wrong—is alien to the ancient climate of opinion, though it surfaces in a few statements by villains in Plato's dialogues.

The theme of justice is first sounded by the poet Hesiod, but comes to enjoy special importance in Athenian tragedy. Anyone who has read Aeschylus' *Oresteia* knows that justice is a major theme in ancient Greek tragedy. Democratic audiences liked to be reminded that tyrants who put themselves above the law are a bane not only to their people but, eventually, to themselves. Such is the message of Sophocles' *Antigone*, for example. Tyrants are often found in these plays, always in trouble, and usually marked by their contempt for justice under law and their *hubris*.

Hubris is the vice of those whose power and success have led them to believe that they know what is best, that they can make good decisions without consultation, and that they have the power to get away with whatever they decide to do. The countervailing virtue is reverence, and the Chorus in a tragedy often celebrates this:

> Wisdom? It's not wise
> To lift our thoughts too high;
> We are human, and our time is short.
> A man who aims at greatness
> Will not live to own what he has now.
> That, I believe, is the life of men
> Who have gone mad and turned
> Their judgment evil. (*Bacchae* 395-402)[11]

This comes from a play by Euripides, the *Bacchae*, but it is a sentiment often encountered in tragic plays. Its specific relevance for democracy derives from its role as an internal restraint in people with power—a restraint that should keep them obedient to law and responsive to advice.

Athenian tragic plays thus had a role in public education, stressing the core values of the democracy. And the Athenians were grateful.

5. Honoring the Music of Democracy

I will close with a story that is a little too good to be true, but much too good not to pass along to you. We are told that the tragic poet Sophocles, after many honors and many victories in the annual contest of plays, lived to a great age. When he was nearly eighty, his sons brought suit to take control of his property, claiming that old age had robbed him of the ability to manage it in a responsible way.

The case came to some sort of trial, probably in 407 BCE, at a time when Sophocles was at work on his final masterpiece, *Oedipus at Colonus*. It is too bad that this play has been eclipsed by the *Antigone* and the other Oedipus play. It is an extraordinary work, and it richly repays a close reading.[12] At its center is a contrast between the tyrannical behavior of a tyrannical Creon and the reverence of Theseus. Creon is the same ruler we met in the *Antigone*, but he is a one-dimensional tyrant in this play. Theseus is the legendary king of Athens, but he was a hero of the democracy, and he tends to carry democratic values in Athenian storytelling. In this play the most striking difference between the two rulers is in their attitude towards the weakest person around. He is a suppliant, a refugee we would call him, an old blind man with a marked limp, who supports himself with a staff and depends on the eyes of a young girl, his daughter. The suppliant is Oedipus. He is not entirely powerless; oracles have told that he has a blessing to confer. Creon is prepared to secure this blessing by violence. Theseus is prepared to help the old man whether he has a blessing to offer or not, simply because it is the right thing for a reverent leader to do.

At his trial on charges of senility, Sophocles recited about 800 lines of the play, or so we are told, a little less than half of the play as we now have it. We don't know which 800 lines he performed, but they sufficed. The poet won his case. We don't know why this demonstration convinced the judges. After all, a gifted poet may still be incompetent at managing his wealth, just as Sophocles' sons charged.

Perhaps the judges were impressed by Sophocles' memory—he had been able to recite a passage of verse that would have lasted over half an hour. Perhaps they were impressed by the quality of the verse—which is magnificent, as we can now see for ourselves. But I would like to think that they were most impressed by the evidence of this play, that this generous spring that had nourished Athens for over 53 years had not run dry, and that Sophocles was still putting forth the music of democracy.

Notes

1. Athens was not, as is often said, a direct democracy. The council (*boulê*) had final say on what could come before the assembly, and legislation had to go through the lawmakers (*nomothetai*) before coming to a vote in the assembly (*ecclesia*). Any citizen could speak or vote in the assembly, although in fact only the first 6000 or so who showed up would be permitted to take part. The best and most detailed account of the workings of Athenian democracy is Mogens German Hansen's.

2. Lincoln's plea for harmony is addressed to the South at his first inauguration:
    We are not enemies, but friends. We must not be enemies. Though passion may have strained, it must not break our bonds of affection. The mystic chords of memory, stretching from every battlefield and patriot grave to every living heart and hearthstone all over this broad land, will yet swell the chorus of the Union when again touched, as surely they will be, by the better angels of our nature. (Lincoln)
3. Most of the scandal that has been spread about Athenian democracy derives from events in the early, more experimental phase. For the best account of the final form of Athenian democracy, see Hansen. In fact, Athenian democracy was highly successful for most of its history. Outbursts of tyranny by the majority were rare in the first hundred years and nonexistent in the second. The democracy would have lasted indefinitely, had the great armies of Macedon and Rome not put it down. The Athenians continued to seethe and rebel in support of democracy until well into the Roman era, so strongly did they feel in favor of their freedoms.
4. The lesson emerged from my work on democracy for my book, *First Democracy: The Challenge of an Ancient Idea.* That book is the source of the ideas in this paper.
5. As our own divisive electoral campaigns dive for the mud, I wonder if we Americans will have to learn the value of harmony the hard way. I hope not.
6. (My translation, for *First Democracy*). The play was written in 411 BCE, at a time when Athenians were eager for peace, and some (at least) were giving up on democracy.
7. From my translation in Meineck and Woodruff 2003. Most scholars now agree that Haemon here speaks for the democratic values of Sophocles himself. See for example Roberts 1994, p. 37.
8. "One day showed us all to be one tribe of humans": Sophocles, from a fragment of a play called *Tereus,* (fragment 591). The "one day" is the day of birth. "What a waste of words it is to speak / In praise of high birth for human beings": Euripides, from a fragment of a play called *Alexander* (fragment 53).
9. Creon, in Sophocles' *Oedipus Tyrannus.*
10. I review the evidence for this in Woodruff, *Reverence: Renewing a Forgotten Virtue.*
11. Euripides' *Bacchae,* from my translation.

12. Peter Meineck's translation in Meineck and Woodruff makes good reading. For an analysis of the play, see my introduction to that edition.
13. This famous couplet, to sophon d'ou sophia/to te mê sophon phronein, uses a play on the two main senses of sophos—wise, clever. "It's not wise to be a wise-ass, or to think oneself beyond the level of a mortal."

Works Cited

Euripides. *Bacchae*. Trans. Paul Woodruff. Indianapolis: Hackett Publishing Company, 1998.

Gagarin, Michael and Paul Woodruff, *Early Greek Political Thought: From Homer to the Sophists.* Cambridge: Cambridge UP, 1995.

Hansen, Mogens German. *The Athenian Democracy in the Age of Demosthenes; Structure, Principles, and Ideology.* Trans. J. A. Crook. 2nd ed. Norman, OK: U of Oklahoma P, 1999.

Lincoln, Abraham. "First Inaugural Address." *The Avalon Project: Documents in Law, History and Diplomacy.* Yale Law School, Lillian Goldman Law Library. <http://avalon.law.yale.edu/19th_century/lincoln1.asp>.

Meineck, Peter, and Paul Woodruff. *Sophocles Theban Plays.* Indianapolis: Hackett Publishing Company, 2003

Roberts, Jennifer Tolbert. *Athens on Trial: The Antidemocratic Tradition on Western Thought.* Princeton: Princeton UP, 1994.

Woodruff, Paul. *First Democracy: The Challenge of an Ancient Idea.* New York: Oxford UP, 2005.

---. Woodruff, *Reverence: Renewing a Forgotten Virtue.* New York: Oxford UP, 2001.

Nature and Tyranny in Aristophanes' *Birds*: The Real Meal Deal

Anne Leavitt
Malaspina University-College

When it comes to sheer personal accomplishment within the world of a fictional drama, it's hard to imagine a character more successful than Pisthetairos, the man who drives the action in Aristophanes' spectacularly over-the-top satire, the *Birds*.[1] Fed up with the litigiousness and artificial constraints of Athenian society, he and a fellow citizen, Euelpides, guided by two rather incoherent birds they acquired in the agora, set out to find Tereus, a man whose crime resulted in his being turned into a hoopoe bird.[2] The two old men hope to discover from Tereus, who has surveyed the earth from a great height, a more congenial place to live. By the end of the play, however, not only has Pisthetairos acquired wings of his own, he has persuaded the free-flying chorus of birds (summoned by Tereus) to stay in one place and to found a city, Cloudcuckooland. Under the direction of Pisthetairos, the birds engineer a complete conquest of the air, and so begins their apparently benign empire extending over both men and gods, and over which the old Pisthetairos, with a stunningly beautiful goddess bride, rules with the power and authority of almighty Zeus. That his friend, Euelpides, leaves the play in a something of a snit early on is something Pisthetairos never so much as notes. But when one chances upon a course that will see one become the ruler of humans, nature and the gods, the loss of one old friend along the way probably doesn't much matter.

Given that this play was performed in 414 BCE, not long after Athens had launched its most ambitious and imperially motivated Sicilian Expedition under the stunning political and military leadership of Alcibiades, one may be tempted to see in the *Birds* Aristophanes' celebration of both. Just as the city of the birds establishes its hegemony over the air through the advanced technology of an amazing wall to control the space between gods and men, so the Athenians held supremacy of the seas with their own long walls and sophisticated navy. And, just as the scheme to extend the Athenian Empire over Sicily would have been unthinkable without the boldness and brilliance of Alcibiades, so the hegemony of the birds would never have been possible without the forethought, persuasion, and boldness of Pisthetairos. Despite the fact that the Sicilian Expedition ended in horrifying failure, and despite the fact that Pisthetairos' fortuitous venture is the stuff of pure fantasy, it is almost impossible not to be swept away with admiration for the sheer spectacle, audacity, and brilliance of both.[3] Unaware of the disaster that would await his fellow citizens in Sicily, could it be that Aristophanes' *Birds* is an invitation to admire and celebrate the boldness, intelligence, and technological sophistication requisite to securing the political prize of benign empire? Is the *Birds* a satire with no target, a pure, unadulterated piece of imperial propaganda?[4]

It would be were it not for one crucial and profoundly disturbing scene. On the brink of ultimate success, when he will acquire by marriage the power and authority of Zeus, Pisthetairos, first of citizens among the birds and possessed of his own feathered wings, has prepared for him in private a fine dinner cooked with cheese and exquisite spices (2035-2045). The feast, we discover, is a feast of birds. Here, in a masterful stroke, Aristophanes presents the otherwise unremarkable act of sitting down to a chicken dinner as an act virtually indistinguishable from cannibalism, and it cannot but stick as a bone in one's throat. After being feasted with the spectacle of a man whose alliance with the birds has allowed for the unparalleled technological conquest of nature for the mutual benefit of both men and birds, we are jolted into wondering whether we really understood anything about the man we have been seduced into admiring, let alone the dark side of his spectacular venture. All along, it appears, we have been cheering the success of a tyrant, a man who would earn the trust and secure the advancement of his fellow citizens only to end up blithely devouring them. From the beginning of the play, it seems, Aristophanes has not been engaged in imperial propaganda but rather in constructing an elaborate joke. And the joke has been on us.

There's a great deal one might say about the *Birds* as a study into the nature and origins of tyranny. For, until his feast (which is not witnessed by the chorus of birds), the tyrant Pisthetairos never appears as a monster.[5] Rather, he presents himself to both the birds and to the audience of the play as the kind of best friend we'd all like to have. Pisthetairos is sensitive to the great fears the birds have of human snares and frying pans (680-700), and he is also sensitive to the ways in which the birds have benefited ungrateful humans since time immemorial by announcing the seasons, prophesying, distributing seeds, and keeping insects at bay (628-632, 659). In answer to their fears and resentment of their human enemies, Pisthetairos proposes that the birds take the place of the Olympian gods. Supported by a new, natural theology articulating their divine status (908-962), and having given up their natural freedom for the concerted organisation of political life, the birds will continue to benefit humans as long as humans acknowledge the divine sovereignty of the birds (770-838). Indeed, the new, natural theology is even bound to appear as far more reasonable to humans beings than the old cosmology of the gods, grounded as the new one is in a great deal of publicly verifiable natural phenomena. As to the wee problem of the Olympians who are not likely to take kindly to being dethroned, the scheme is simple. Under the orders of Pisthetairos, the birds build a wall that prevents the smoke of sacrifices from reaching the gods (220-234). The hunger of the Olympians forces them to sue for peace (1960-1970). Who wouldn't want someone like Pisthetairos on their side? The fact that he stores a harmless cooking pot and barbeque spit in Tereus' kitchen early on in the play (550) is not something that we or the birds find in any way remarkable at the time. Successful tyrants, Aristophanes suggests, tend to appear as their opposites—the best gift a community could ever hope for. They appeal to the same natural desire we share with the birds, the desire to avoid being devoured by others. The complete fulfillment of that desire, however, requires imperial dominion over all actual and potential threats. Pisthetairos, the tyrant, is the kind of leader who can satisfy this need for imperial dominion in the name of public safety precisely because he recognises no moral limits to his own aspirations. He is, indeed, the kind of man who can devour his fellow citizens without a second thought. While appearing as the answer to their every dream, he is, in fact, their worst nightmare.[6]

In fact, it is precisely the moral limits placed on human behaviour by civil society that lead Pisthetairos and his friend Euelpides to abandon Athens in the first place and to throw in their lot with the birds.[7] And, certainly the ways of the birds cannot help but appear as extremely attractive. The birds are all equals, and they are all equally free.[8] They have no need of laws, including laws against father beating (1000), and they have no need for money (190-193). They are beautiful, and their wings allow them free access to any place in the world (270-300). They are also beneficent in so far as they play an integral role in the cyclical economy of the earth (1355-1370). The ways of the birds are supremely natural; they acknowledge none of the restrictions associated with human civil life.[9] While the birds turn to Pisthetairos in order to secure their safety, Pisthetairos and Euelpides turn to the birds for the sake of freedom, the freedom made possible by a life lived in accordance with nature that is not possible in civil society. That such a life is indeed not possible in civil society is illustrated, of course, by the fate of the birds themselves. Their conquest of men and gods requires that they organise themselves into a community. Not only does that require the rule of law[10] and the sacrifice of individual freedom for the sake of a collective enterprise[11], but it also requires the leadership of the brilliant Pisthetairos who rules, not as an equal, but as their superior.[12]

The *Birds* that is, presents not just one but two profound ironies, and they are clearly connected. On the one hand, we are invited to consider the profound irony in the ways that successful tyrants appear to their communities as their opposite. On the other hand, we are also invited to consider the ways in which the ways of nature can serve as the ways of a community only to the extent that they are de-natured.[13] The connection between these two ironies is found in the figure of Pisthetairos. Pisthetairos is supremely attracted to the life of nature and repelled by the life of civil society. And he establishes his rule over the entire cosmos by both an alliance with and promotion of nature as the ultimate standard for both humans and the gods. In so doing, however, he must actually transform the natural ways of the birds into the ways of civil life. Pisthetairos thereby realises his own dream; he does acquire the freedom and power to live his own life in accordance with the ways of nature. The rest of the cosmos, however, is not so fortunate. Pisthetairos, by the end of the play, is in a position to devour all he wishes with impunity.

The further irony in this, of course, is that this too is supremely natural. While the attractiveness of the life of nature as presented in this play lies in its lawlessness, freedom, and beauty, it should not be ignored that nature, in this play, is also the source of food. Food, in fact, is the glue that holds much of the drama together. When Euelpides and Pisthetairos first meet the birds, they are carrying a cook pot and a barbeque spit. The birds, of course, initially regard both men as the natural enemies they are and threaten, not only to attack, but also to eat them (410-422). The birds resent the fact that humans consider them to be delicious delicacies (693-702), and part of their promise to humans who worship them is a secure supply of food (789-790, 1355-1370). Further, not only are the gods forced to sue for peace when deprived of the sustenance of sacrifices (2045), in one of the most hilarious moments of the play, it is clear that the savoury odour of the fowl that Pisthetairos is about to eat contributes to the gluttonous god Heracles' willingness to sacrifice his birthright (2245-2250). Pisthetairos, that is, not only acquires the freedom and power to live his life in accordance with the ways of nature, he does so because he understands the fundamental law of nature. As Stephen Sondheim's Sweeny Todd puts it: "The history of the world, my sweet, is who gets eaten and who gets to eat."[14] It is, after all, due to the fact that Pisthetairos secures control over the cosmic food chain that he manages to win his empire. From the point of view of nature, there's nothing unnatural about that.

Indeed, it is both the dependence of humans on nature and the dependence of gods on humans that allow Pisthetairos to flip the traditional order of the cosmos.[15] While it might appear that the gods are the natural superiors of humans and that humans are the natural superiors of the natural world, Pisthetairos understands that without the bounty of nature, humans are nothing, and without humans to worship them, the gods would wither and die.[16] By exploiting these natural dependencies, Pisthetairos appears to restore a rational and natural order to things—the world of nature, namely the birds, will rule both gods and humans. The irony here, of course, is that it is not really nature in the form of the birds that rules at the end of the *Birds*, but the man-bird Pisthetairos, who has made himself a god, upon whom nature, humans, and gods depend. And he, like Mother Nature herself, has no scruples when it comes to devouring his own.

In a remarkable scene in the play, a sycophant (one of the many humans who wish to join the city of the birds) asks Pisthetairos for wings so that he can fly around in search of potential law suits (1751 ff). Not only does Pisthetairos order the man to find a more lawful occupation, he tells him that he needs no wings. As he says, "With words all men can give themselves their wings"(1788), and "With words our minds are raised—a man can soar."(1795) Within the world of the play, of course, Pisthetairos is absolutely right. Although he himself acquires wings early on, he never needs to use them.[17] Pisthetairos' conquest of the cosmos has been achieved by words alone. It is not by military force, but by persuading the birds with "winged words" to fall in with his schemes, that Pisthetairos succeeds.[18]

In his play, Aristophanes shows us how the appeal of winged words, which promise the freedom and security, which humans crave by nature, can be used to enslave them. Wielded by a man who takes the law of nature, and not the moral constraints of civil society or the will of the gods, as his standard, such winged words may be right in exposing the degree to which civil constraints and traditional ways of looking at things are limiting, unnatural, and may even be undone. A community that follows such a man for the sake of public safety and glory, however, is a community on a path that leads to slavery. The top of the food chain is not a position that is easily shared. It is inconceivable that a community could ever have more than one successful Pisthetairos in its midst.[19] And, as he well knows, "The history of the world, my sweet, is who gets eaten and who gets to eat."

Notes

1. I am indebted to Ian Johnston, a recently retired colleague, for his marvellous new translation of this play. As Ian has taught me, one of the motors that drives a successful satire and, indeed, all good jokes, is that the audience's conventional expectations concerning such things as language, plot, and character types are constantly undermined in delightfully surprising ways (which is one of the reasons, for instance, that we laugh out loud at the spectacle of a pretentious politician slipping on a banana-peel as he nears the podium to deliver a serious speech.) While there have been many marvellous translations of Aristophanes' plays over the years, one of the problems students often have with many of them is the out datedness of much of the language. Words used to translate Aristophanes' insults, and sexual and scatological references, for instance, while somewhat shocking to audiences of a previous generation, tend to strike one as both tame and euphemistic today.

Ian's translations of Aristophanes' plays, while as faithful to the original Greek as can be, are attempts to render Aristophanes' humour into idioms more appropriate for a 21st century audience raised with the explicitness of modern television. Not only do his translations preserve much of the laugh-out-loud flavour of the Greek originals; arguably, given the rawness of much of Aristophanes' humour, the idioms of 21st century English more accurately translate the language of Aristophanes than has been possible in the past. Ian has made his translations of Aristophanes' plays (along with a host of other translated material) available for use by the public at his web site <http://www.mala.bc.ca/~johnstoi/>. All references to the *Birds* in this paper are drawn from Ian's translation.

2. Tereus was a legendary king of Thrace. He married Procne and raped her sister, Philomena. In revenge, the two sisters killed Tereus' son and fed Tereus the remains for dinner. All three were turned into birds: Tereus into a hoopoe, Procne into a nightingale, and Philomena into a swallow. By the end of the play, it becomes clear that the story of Tereus foreshadows much of the outcome.

3. Thucydides' description of the magnificence of the Athenian fleet as it set sail for Sicily, and the awe it inspired, may be found in 6.31 of his *History of the Peloponnesian War*.

4. This view is espoused by the popular Perseus Project's on-line *Perseus Encylopedia*, which may be found at <http://www.perseus.tufts.edu>. Under the heading "Aristophanes (2)," one finds the claim that "Aristophanes was a sharp observer of the social and political life of Athens, but his plays reveal no systematic or original political credos. In *Archeries* and *Lysistrata* the sympathetic characters denounce the folly and greed of Athens' wartime leaders and urge that more should be done to negotiate a peaceful settlement, but *Birds* supports vigorous prosecution of the war-effort, particularly the expedition against Sicily." A more common reading of the *Birds* is outlined by Moses Hadas in his general introduction to *The Complete Plays of Aristophanes*. Hadas maintains that the *Birds* has no specific target but is rather a "utopian fantasy" prompted by the "sad state of the human condition" (9). In his introductory note to the *Birds* itself, Hadas claims that "[The *Birds*] attacks no specific abuse but is literally escapist . . ." (229). This paper rejects both positions.

5. Indeed, nothing in the play suggests that the birds ever see Pisthetairos for the monster he is. Unlike the audience of the play, the birds don't actually get to see him prepare his feast of birds. It's only after hearing that Pisthetairos will gain the power and authority of Zeus when he marries the goddess Sovereignty that their song becomes uncharacteristically sombre as they sing of humans who have committed various crimes (1910 ff, 2008 ff, 2255 ff). Perhaps, at this moment, they begin to divine that Pisthetairos may supplant them as gods in the eyes of men. Their final song, however, is one of great joy at Pisthetairos' marriage (2305 ff).
6. In his initial efforts to gain the trust of the birds, Pisthetairos sympathetically sums up the humiliation of the birds by humans this way:
If you seem good to eat,
they don't simply roast you by yourself—no!
They grate on cheese, mix oil and silphium
with vinegar—and then whip up a sauce,
oily and sweet, which they pour on you hot,
as if you were a chunk of carrion meat. (689-701)
It is a delicious irony that, as the play describes in great detail, this is precisely the recipe Pisthetairos himself later chooses for preparing his own feast of birds.
7. While both men want to escape the litigiousness of Athens, Euelpides also longs for a life where he can find himself invited to partake of a wedding banquet and never have to help out the host should the host find himself in financial trouble. Pisthetairos also dreams of the day the father of a lovely boy will approach him to complain that Pisthetairos has not lavished sufficient amorous attentions on the man's son (150-170).
8. Their wings are the source of their freedom (1040).
9. As the birds explain to humans, "Here, you see, whatever is considered shameful by your laws, is all just fine among us birds" (999-1000).
10. We are told that the birds that Pisthetairos is preparing to eat were condemned to death for political insurgency against the birds' democracy (2040).
11. The building of the walls is carried out by the birds themselves. This requires a high degree of organisation, the division of labour, and intensely concerted effort (1450-1482).
12. The birds make it clear that they require the intelligence and direction of Pisthetairos if the scheme is to succeed (850).

13. The de-naturing of the birds has, of course, begun long before Pisthetairos and Euelipes meet them. Tereus, we learn, has long ago taught them how to speak (240). It's also worth noting that Tereus has living with him a servant who, like Tereus, was a man but has been turned into a bird. When asked by Euelpides, "Does a bird need his own butler bird?" the servant-bird responds, *"He* does—I think it's got something to do with the fact that earlier he was a man" (90). By the end of the play, Pisthetairos has a few servants of his own.
14. According to Thucydides, a version of this law of nature was appealed to by the Athenians as justification for their destruction of the people of Melos in 416 BCE, two years before the *Birds* was performed *(History of the Peloponnesian War,* 5.85-113). And, according to Thucydides, Alcibiades later appealed to this law to justify the Sicilian Expedition: " . . . if we desist in ruling others, we risk being ruled ourselves" (6.18).
15. The overthrow of the traditional order of the cosmos is prefigured by the site on which the city of the birds is to be built, the Phlegra Plain, where, according to Pisthetairos, "gods beat up on all the giants in a bragging match" (1090-1100). The reference is to the overthrow of the Titans by the Olympians. It's no accident that Prometheus shows up towards the end of this play to help Pisthetairos out.
16. Pisthetairos insists that the famine caused by the wall will annihilate the gods (220 ff). He also insists that it is possible for the goddess, Iris, to die (1549). Pisthetairos does not appear to believe in the immortality of the gods.
17. Pisthetairos uses his wings only at the very end of the play when he flies to Heaven for his wedding.
18. In likening words to wings when he speaks to the sycophant, Pisthetairos may well be speaking from immediate, personal experience in more than the obvious sense. It's not at all clear that he planned his take-over of the cosmos from the beginning (though he clearly has what it takes to pull it off.) Rather, he appears to improvise a great deal as he goes along, taking advantage of opportunities as they come up (his marriage to the goddess, Sovereignty, for instance, was never premeditated. Prometheus who just "happens" to show up suggests the marriage to him. Pisthetairos doesn't even know who this goddess is until Prometheus tells him.) It's worth wondering the extent to which Pisthetairos' own words

run ahead of him, as it were, and cause his own mind "to rise" as he formulates them. He is a born talker, bursting with words. As he says, just before he delivers his first big speech to the chorus of birds, "By god, I'm full of words, bursting to speak. I've worked my speech like well-mixed flour—\like kneading dough. There's nothing stopping me."(581). Not only is it interesting that Pisthetairos likens his rising words to bread, an important source of sustenance, the analogy suggests they have a kind of rising power that is independent of him, and all their own, once he lets them go.

19. It is highly significant that Euelpides leaves the play about halfway through and never returns. While he does not harbour the same political ambitions as Pisthetairos, he nonetheless seems to see where Pisthetairos' scheme may lead. It is when Pisthetairos peremptorily orders Euelpides to aid the birds in constructing the wall that Euelpides balks (1118-1122). He's miffed at the suggestion that he should work while Pisthetairos remains behind. Euelpides stays true to his desire for the natural life of freedom and sees that this is incompatible with taking orders from Pisthetairos. The authentically free man-bird that Euelpides has become, however, will have no home, having exiled himself from both Athens and the city of the birds.

Works Cited

Aristophanes. *Birds.* Johnston, Ian. trans. Malaspina University-College, Nanaimo, BC, 2004. <http://records.viu.ca/~johnstoi/aristophanes/birds.htm>.

Hadas, Moses. Introduction. *The Complete Plays of Aristophanes* New York: Bantam Books Classic Edition, 1981.

Thucydides. *History of the Peloponnesian War.* Trans. Martin Hammond. Oxford: Oxford's World Classics, 2009.

Lyric Breath: Taking Seriously the Trope of Immortality in Shakespeare's *Sonnets*

Scott F. Crider
University of Dallas

> [R]eading engages the reader with the community
> in the interest of the immortality of all persons.
>
> Allen Grossman[1]

Shakespeare's Speaker opens the sonnet sequence with a universal claim about the human relationship with mortal beauty: "From fairest creatures we desire increase, / That thereby beauty's rose might never die" (1.1-2).[2] Animated by that desire for increase, the Speaker continually appeals to the trope of poetic immortality: his sonnets immortalize his beloved.[3] Readers and critics often discount the appeal, given that, as every wag likes to point out, no one knows who the Fair Youth is.[4] That misses the point, I think. In the mimetic world of *Shakespeare's Sonnets*, something is saved, after all, though we do not know exactly what that is. To take seriously a trope which, by the sequence's publication in 1609, was already fatigued makes it possible to discern our Speaker's distinct conception of the trope, a conception which provides a definition of lyric as an act of saving one's own love within a lyric expression whose very recitation across time makes real a presence which is not simply the poet's, the speaker's or the reader's alone, but also another's, even if that *other* were to turn out to be fictive. *Shakespeare's Sonnets* ask us to consider someone else's love—both as object and as experience—*as* our own as we read the poems. There are any number of metaphors in the sequence for the process of lyric composition—conceiving (1.1-4), distilling (5.9-14 and 54.13-14), grafting (15.13-14), and printing (65.13-14), for example. I would like to concentrate on one metaphor for the process of lyric *reading*—that of breathing—in order to reveal the Speaker's mission to orchestrate the performance—not in silent reading, but in oral recitation—of his beloved's reanimation once both speaker and beloved are dead. The reader can breathe life into that other—establishing presence where only absence appears—through the act of reading aloud, one's breath the instrument of the reanimation.[5] The reader's voice is the instrument of the music of the poem. If one takes the claim seriously, the interpretive consequences are significant: The sequence's mission is neither strictly Orphic, nor strictly Christian, though informed by both; instead, it is distinctly modern, our Speaker seeking a strictly human transcendence over finitude by means of lyric. If the Speaker's mission is serious, reading lyric poetry aloud establishes a community whose members are not limited to the living.

Let me examine Sonnet 81's distinct form of the trope of immortality—reading aloud as the reanimation of the dead beloved through the breath of the reader—then the poem's Biblical intertext in *Genesis*, and the interpretive consequences of the sonnet's and the sequence's appropriation of a hitherto divine power. First, the poem:

> Or I shall live, your epitaph to make;
> Or you survive, when I in earth am rotten;
> From hence your memory death cannot take,
> Although in me each part will be forgotten.
> Your name from hence immortal life shall have,
> Though I, once gone, to all the world must die;
> The earth can yield me but a common grave,
> When you entombed in men's eyes shall lie.
> Your monument shall be my gentle verse,
> Which eyes not yet created shall o'er-read;
> And tongues to be your being shall rehearse,
> When all the breathers of this world are dead.

Taking Seriously the Trope of Immortality in Shakespeare's Sonnets 99

> You still shall live, such virtue hath my pen,
> Where breath most breathes, even in the mouths of men.

Once both Speaker and Fair Youth are dead, the Fair Youth "entombed in men's eyes shall lie" (8) in the "gentle verse" monumentalizing him, verse which the eyes of future readers shall "o'er-read." Notice that the eyes of future readers are entombing the Fair Youth, preserving him, yet preserving him in a dead state. Potential for life is achieved by the published poem; actualization of life, though, requires not only reading with one's eyes, then, but also speaking with one's mouth, here figured as both tongue and breath:

> And **tongues** / to **be**, // your **be**/ing **shall** / **rehearse**,
> When **all** / the **brea**/thers of / **this world** / are **dead**.
> You **still** / **shall live**, // such **vir**/tue **hath** / my **pen**,
> Where **breath** / most **breathes**, / ev'n in / the **mouths** / of **men**.[6]

The tongue as synecdoche for speech itself is common in the period. In Thomas Wilson's *Art of Rhetoric*, for example, he explains rhetorical delivery thus: "The tongue giveth a certain grace to every matter and beautifieth the cause in like manner as a sweet-sounding lute much setteth forth a mean-devised ballad" (242). Ultimately, these "tongues to be" will not entomb the Fair Youth, but "shall rehearse" his "being." The Speaker is clearly imagining oral delivery: to "rehearse" is to recite aloud.[7] Notice that the Speaker is no longer promising that the Fair Youth's "name" will have "immortal life"; now, readers will rehearse his "being." How will they do so, exactly; that is, what is the agent of the immortality? It is, of course, the "virtue," or excellence of, the poet's pen. That is a virtue which depends upon the breath of rehearsal, though. Breathers contemporary with the Speaker and the Fair Youth—"all the breathers of *this world*"—no doubt rehearse that "being," but the Speaker is attempting to achieve not only fame within their own cultural world, but also immortality beyond it, though not Christian eternity beyond the world itself.[8] The Fair Youth "still shall live . . . / Where breath most breathes, even in the mouths of men." The figure now is not the tongue, but breath, the breath of life which in Shakespeare's Geneva Bible is the divine action of inaugurating human life: "The Lord God also made the man of dust of the ground, and breathed in his face the breath of life, and the man was a living soul" (Genesis 2.7). God Himself gives life by breathing the breath of life into inanimate dust, thus animating him as a living soul. The Speaker's claim is extraordinary. He is positing an associative action between the Speaker and the oral reader, both of whom are exercising together a power hitherto reserved to God: making a living soul. The virtue of the Speaker's pen is to fashion a textual body which, once read aloud, breathes life into the text, the "being" of the Fair Youth "still" living in the present moment of lyric rehearsal in—that is, "by means of"—"the mouths of men," including that moment now in the mouth of this breather of the poem.[9]

How seriously shall we take this scandalous claim by Shakespeare's Speaker? I recommend very seriously. I have found that when I read poems aloud, and when I hear others do so, our voices change, become in some way *other*, even as they rehearse other worlds and persons. I do not know exactly what is present in my voice, but I would suggest that it is perhaps a trace of the Speaker's voice to the Fair Youth. In such delivery, I am speaking to a degree *as* the Speaker *of* a presence that is somehow, in the speaking, brought forward. Until I have a better explanation of what occurs during that lyric moment and how it does so, I must allow the possibility that I am reanimating the Speaker and the Fair Youth through breathing what the Speaker's penned, who both then become, during the recital, living souls. This claim is a scandal, but it is the Speaker's claim. Even a sonnet so apparently well known as Sonnet 18 turns out to house a more radical claim about the community of the living and the dead than the millions of students who have learned the poem realize since they so seldom, unfortunately, read the entire sequence. Sonnet 18, especially its couplet, waits for Sonnet 81, indeed the full sonnet sequence, to explain, defend and even qualify its scandalous claim:

> Shall I compare thee to a summer's day?
> Thou art more lovely and more temperate:
> Rough winds do shake the darling buds of May,
> And summer's lease hath all too short a date:
> Sometime too hot the eye of heaven shines,
> And often is his gold complexion dimm'd,
> And every fair from fair sometime declines,
> By chance, or nature's changing course untrimm'd:
> But thy eternal summer shall not fade,
> Nor lose possession of that fair thou ow'st,
> Nor shall death brag thou wander'st in his shade,
> When in eternal lines to time thou grow'st:
> So long as men can breathe or eyes can see,
> So long lives this, and this gives life to thee.[10]

Notes

1. *Summa Lyrica* 1.7 in *The Sighted Singer: Two Works on Poetry for Readers and Writers* by Allen Grossman with Mark Halliday, 205-383, 213.
2. All citations from the sequence are from Katherine Duncan Jone's 3rd Arden edition. But I have profitably consulted Stephen Booth's edition and commentary, 275-9.
3. Of course, this trope disappears after the Fair Youth sonnets (1-126). I will address only the first beloved in the sequence, not the second, the relationship of the two of which is a topic too large to examine here.
4. In *Shakespeare's Perjured Eye*, Joel Fineman makes a more subtle indictment of the trope, that praise of the beloved is actually always self-praise: "[P]raise is an objective showing that is essentially subjective showing off" (6). It is true that this may be the case, but I cannot see why it must always be so. As well, even if true, this would alter only the object of the saving, not the fact of it.
5. George T. Wright has argued in "The Silent Speech of Shakespeare's Sonnets" that the sonnets are "at least equally appropriately read without sound" (137). The Speaker would not, I think, agree.
6. I have bolded syllables to indicate relative stress. The trochaic "ev'n in" makes audible the extent of the accomplishment. See 116.12 for the same medial troche, "ev'n to."
7. Booth points out that "rehearse" can mean either "recite" or "recount," adding that there may be a play on re-hearse, to bury again (278).
8. This is a conceptual difference the speaker does not often acknowledge, often using "eternity" when he should use "immortality." See, for example, 38.11-12. Eternity encompasses a time after Judgment, but immortality does not; eternity is a Judeo-Christian concept, but immortality a Greco-Roman one. As the Speaker acknowledges in 53.13-14: "So till the judgment that yourself arise / You live in this, and dwell in lovers' eyes." Whether Shakespeare is treating his Speaker with irony—that is, undercutting the project of immortalization—is very difficult, perhaps impossible, to determine.
9. Helen Vendler puts this well in *The Art of Shakespeare's Sonnets*: "[B]y the invention of memorial *utterance* as well as memorial

reading, the poet and the young man together are given perpetual spoken life by posterity until the end of time" (363).
10. I would like to thank the other members of the ACTC panel on the lyric: Louise Cowan, Robert Dupree, Eileen Gregory, who introduced me to Allen Grossman's work, and Bernadette Waterman Ward, who delivered the paper in my absence. Gerard Wegemer provided a characteristically helpful reading of the text.

Works Cited

Allen Grossman. *The Sighted Singer: Two Works on Poetry for Readers and Writers*. Baltimore and London: John Hopkins UP, 1992.

Fineman, Joel. *Shakespeare's Perjured Eye*. Berkeley: U of California P, 1986.

The Geneva Bible: A facsimile of the 1560 edition. Intro. Lloyd E. Berry. Madison: U of Wisconsin P, 1969. Spelling modernized.

Shakespeare, William. Sonnets. Ed. Stephen Booth. New Haven and London: Yale UP, 1977.

---. Sonnets. Ed. Katherine Duncan Jone. 3rd ed. London: Thomas Publishing Company, 1997.

Vendler, Helen. *The Art of Shakespeare's Sonnets*. Cambridge, Mass.: Harvard UP, 1997.

Wilson, Thomas. *Art of Rhetoric*. Ed. Peter Medine. Park, Pennsylvania: Pennsylvania UP, 1994.

Whose Underground?: Notes on Locating Dostoyevsky

Margaret Heller
University of King's College

While many disciplines in the humanities are organized according to nationality, liberal arts or core text programs are often organized according to civilization: to the West first of all but increasingly to other civilizations, those belonging to the somewhat mysterious and indefinable "nonWest." Such divisions are, of course, to some extent merely convenient. There has to be some principle of arrangement of a curriculum, and we can recognize that any grouping will not be exact. It seems increasingly clear, however, that classification according to civilization is questionable: cultural contact and exchange means civilizations don't form isolated wholes. It is obvious, for example, that European explorations and conquests had an impact on those they encountered, but the effects were not in one direction only. The influence of India on the Baroque decorative arts, of Africa on Baroque music, of China on Enlightenment economic theory, of Japan on Heidegger, and of the Indian caste structure on English society, are among many indications that Western civilization as we commonly understand it has not been merely formed by an unfolding according to an internal logic. Perhaps it is time to give up the concept of civilization altogether and find different categories for analyzing culture.

On the other hand, there are grounds for believing that more fundamental differences between civilizations that are not reconcilable persist despite interconnections on the levels of material and high culture. Perhaps, while there have been significant cultural exchanges, the real structures that define civilizations have remained untouched. The argument for cultural incommensurability has been made most famously in recent years by Samuel P. Huntington through his notion of the " clash of civilizations." In his book of that name he distinguishes, for example, the Western and Hispanic civilizations, and he elaborates upon this typology in a controversial article in the 2004 March/April issue of *Foreign Policy,* in which he worries that a distinctively American civilization, which he believes is Anglo-Protestant, is under threat by the inundation of Hispanic immigration.

Huntington's views find support from a quarter he might find surprising, Julia Kristeva, a poststructuralist theorist. Born in Bulgaria but based in France since the 1960s, Kristeva is a practicing psychoanalyst as well as a linguist and literary and political theorist. In her paper "Europe Divided: Politics, Ethics, Religion," published in *The Crisis of the European Subject* in 2000, Kristeva analyzes the barriers to integration as countries formerly belonging to Eastern Europe are incorporated into the European Union. While the formal negotiations concerning these barriers have revolved around reconciling economic and political differences, Kristeva argues for the importance of thinking how to reconcile the different cultural memories which structure subjectivity. Like Plato, Kristeva believes that the structure of the psyche and the structure of the *polis* mirror one another. Unlike Plato, she is interested in identifying different rather than common structures, and she explains these to a large extent through divergent religious histories. For, despite the apparent disaffection with organized religion in contemporary Europe, Kristeva argues that "religious traditions remain alive and well. They influence—in a way that is subterranean, unconscious—the way of life, the customs, the mentalities, and the decisive attitudes of subjects in the political and economic organization of their society" (132).

The fundamental divide between East and West in the Christian religious tradition began, of course, in 1054 over the relation of the persons of the Trinity. In the Latin West, the Holy Ghost proceeds from the Father *and* the Son (*filioque*), while in the Orthodox East he proceeds from the father *through* the Son (*per filium*). To give a simplistic account of Kristeva's rather complicated argument, the Catholic Trinity, by putting the Son on an equal footing with the Father, makes possible the later Western belief in autonomy of the human subject. The Orthodox Trinity, on the other hand, treats the Son as subordinate to the Father, as a servant who is raised and deified through his servitude; such a conception creates in the believer irresolvable desires to both unite with and separate from the Father rather than the preconditions for psychic autonomy. Unlike the Western Trinity, which allows for the development of individualism and "personalism," the Orthodox trinity encourages what Kristeva calls "an exquisite logic of submission and exaltation" (139).

Kristeva is particularly interested in tracing how this fundamental division results in two distinct paths for modern subjective freedom to emerge in the late eighteenth century. In the West, Kant claimed that the human subject is free because rational, the source of moral law, and thus self-determining. At the same time in Russia, the Hesychastic ("the silence of peace of the union with God") tradition was revived; it held that the human subject is free insofar as the intellect is displaced in favor of the heart. The individual soul is characterized as yearning for universal communion, as needing to go beyond the boundaries of individuation rather than as seeking self-sufficiency. And, because God is experienced without concept, in the order of experience anything is permitted: destruction and sensual intimacy, "negative violence and adoration" (142). Thus, Kristeva argues, the Russians have excelled in the literature of hell (150).

Let us turn to turn to a great example of such literature: Dostoyevsky's *Notes from the Underground*. If Kristeva is right about the fundamental differences between the Western and Orthodox ideas of freedom and even structures of personality, then perhaps we should call into question our habit of including Dostoyevsky in curricula based on the Western tradition. The core text programme to which I belong has often taught Dostoyevsky and other nineteenth-century Russian authors as a matter of course, yet authors such as Frantz Fanon have been added more recently only as the result of a conscious choice to open up the curriculum to include voices from outside the West. I notice that the St. John's curriculum, which is also explicitly centered on the Western tradition, also includes Dostoyevsky.

It is odd that we and they do so, given that Dostoyevsky is so critical of the West. Indeed, as Christopher GoGwilt argues in his *Invention of the West: Joseph Conrad and the Double Mapping of Europe and Empire,* our very conception of being Western is in large part the result of disputes within Russia over its distinction from Europe. The Cold

War opposition between the Western and Eastern Blocs, GoGwilt claims, only "consolidated a process whereby an evolving Russian debate about Europe helped redefine European culture and history" (227). In his *Diary of a Writer*, Dostoyevsky prophesizes that the time will come when Europe will ask Russia to save her from catastrophe. He writes: "She is going to tell us that we too are Europe; that, consequently, we have exactly the same "order of things" as she; that not in vain have we imitated her during two hundred years, boasting that we were Europeans, and that by saving her, we are thereby saving ourselves . . . then, perhaps, for the first time, all of us would grasp at once to what extent all the while we did not resemble Europe, despite our two-hundred year craving for, and dreams about becoming Europe—dreams which used to reach the proportions of passionate fits" (258-9).

It seems clear from this that Dostoyevsky sharply distinguished Russia from Europe, and as a result that we should read his *Notes from the Underground* as an anti-Western text. Its unnamed narrator is a figure of the deracinated westernized intellectual, one who has lost touch with his Russian soul. At the end of the story, he ascribes his moral corruption to his condition as a member of the intelligentsia: "we are all divorced from life, we are all cripples, every one of us, more or less . . . . Why, we have come almost to looking upon real life as an effort, almost as hard work, and we are all privately agreed that it is better in books" (90); "Leave us alone without books and we shall be lost and in confusion at once. We shall not know what to join on to, what to cling to, what to hate, what to respect, and what to despise" (91). The Underground Man's critique of the Crystal Palace is aimed specifically at westernizer Nicolai Chernyshevsky's utilitarian socialist utopia as portrayed in his *What Is To Be Done?*, but it is also aimed generally against the whole Western project of pursuing and maximizing happiness through enlightened self-interest, whether that happiness is to be found in "prosperity, wealth, freedom, peace" (14). In his famous argument, the Underground Man states that obeying the dictates of reason is a form of slavery to necessity, and that human beings' real interest is in being completely free, in following "our own sweet will" no matter how disadvantageous or destructive the results. Indeed, he asks: "Does not man, perhaps, love something besides well-being? Perhaps he is just as fond of suffering? Perhaps suffering is just a great a benefit to him as well-being? Mankind is sometimes extraordinarily, passionately, in love with suffering and that's a fact" (23). It is only by giving up Western ideals and accepting suffering that one can again experience "real life."

In a recent book called *Occidentalism: the West in the Eyes of its Enemies,* Ian Buruma and Avishai Margalit argue that Dostoyevsky is an exponent of "Occidentalism"—a false and negative generalization of the West in parallel, of course, to how Orientalism views the East. They argue that "It is against this Crystal Palace that Dostoyevsky's man of the underground protests. He is convinced that the West is committed to scientism, the belief that society can be engineered like the Crystal Palace. For him, imported scientism and utilitarianism constitute a dangerously deluded ideology . . . . We might share Dostoyevsky's view of human behavior, but his view of the West as a huge Crystal Palace, driven by nothing but arid rationalism, is a dehumanizing Occidentalist distortion" (98).

Yet this characterization of Dostoyevsky as merely anti-Western doesn't really work. For being Western is not something foreign or external to the Underground Man—it is written in his soul, to the extent that he and other of Dostoyevsky's characters experience themselves as split. That is, the West has been taken into the Russian soul and cannot be excised. Again, in his *Diary of a Writer,* Dostoyevsky denies that it would be possible or even desirable to try to return to the way Russia was before the westernizing reforms of Peter the Great. Dostoyevsky's sense is that, while the intelligentsia for two centuries deserted Russia in their hearts, they are now returning; they are returning after their European sojourn not as Europeans, but as cosmopolitans, ready to further Russia's world-historical mission. He writes that "under no circumstances can we renounce Europe. Europe is our second fatherland, and I am the first ardently to profess this; I have always professed this" (581).

Thus, while there are good reasons to think that *Notes from the Underground* is anti-Western, the story is, after all, not a polemic but is narrated through a series of paradoxes, and as such, it is very difficult for the reader to find the bottom line. The Underground Man as a westernized intellectual is not just an object of Dostoyevsky's critique, for he is represented as a figure of possibility as well, as one whose condition is in some way affirmed. He says that, "Though I have said that I envy the normal man to the last drop of my bile, yet I should not care to be in his place such as he is now (though I shall not cease from envying him)" (25). And, "Though I did lay it down at the beginning that consciousness is the greatest misfortune for man, yet I know man prizes it and will not give it up for any satisfaction" (24). Despite its costs, the self-consciousness of the Russian who has encountered Europe is a gift. Dostoyevsky had argued in his *Diary of a Writer* that the Russian Westernizers, insofar as they had joined up with the extreme left in Europe, had become Europe's negators and were thus unconsciously and unintentionally revealing their Russian souls; in a similar way the Slavophiles, including Dostoyevsky even in his most slavophilic moments, could not help revealing their European souls.

Even more, it is possible that Dostoyevsky, although belonging outside the West, also has a place in the Western tradition, for just as Russia took in European thought, so Europe took in Dostoyevsky's novels. Kristeva argues that the West loves the nineteenth-century Russian novelists because they reveal a dimension of the human personality that does not seem available from within the Western tradition proper. Dostoyevsky enlarged the underground of Western culture, by revealing depths not experienced before.

Indeed, where Kristeva departs from Huntington is that she believes that civilizations will change through contact with one another. She hope and expects that the incorporation of formerly "Eastern" European countries into Western Europe will benefit both by bringing together alternative conceptions of human freedom, each one of which can correct a deficiency in the psychic inheritance of the other. In general, Kristeva sees the challenge of reconciliation currently facing Europe as a test case, as a first taste, of the process of globalization that will require that individuals find ways of accommodating themselves to even more disparate structures of subjectivity. It seems to me that the problems facing the US with the increase of Hispanic immigration that so worry Samuel Huntington are hardly extreme examples of this challenge, for they repeat the more familiar problems of reconciling Protestantism and Catholicism. A greater challenge evidently will be to discover how Western nations can accommodate Islam within themselves, and how Islamic nations can accommodate what is Western.

Perhaps we who study the tradition of the West want to read Dostoyevsky, then, not in order to recognize ourselves through our particular "roots," but in order to discover how our particular tradition took something in that was not otherwise available. Perhaps "defamiliarization" should be the real task of liberal education.

A final note. If this is true of reading the novels of Dostoyevsky, it also might be true of works written by others we think of as belonging to the non-West. Much of what gets characterized as postcolonial literature also attempts to negotiate the dilemmas that result from the encounter of modernity and tradition. If Dostoyevsky is to remain part of the Western canon, we need to rethink the boundaries we have erected between the Western and non-Western.

Works Cited

Buruma, Ian, and Avishai Margalit. *Occidentalism: The West in the Eyes of Its Enemies.* New York: Penguin, 2004.

Dostoyevsky, Fyodor. *The Diary of a Writer.* Trans Boris Brasol. 2 vols. New York: Octagon, 1973.

---. *Notes from the Underground.* Trans. Constance Garnett. New York: Dover, 1992.

GoGwilt, Christopher Lloyd. *The Invention of the West: Joseph Conrad and the Double-Mapping of Europe and Empire.* Stanford: Stanford UP, 1995.

Huntington, Samuel P. *The Clash of Civilizations and the Remaking of the World Order.* New York: Touchstone, 1996.

---. "The Hispanic Challenge." *Foreign Policy.* March/April 2004: 30-45.

Kristeva, Julia. *Crisis of the European Subject.* New York: Other Press, 2000.

Community: New Perspectives

Art, Integrating Disciplines, and Liberal Education: Imagining the Possible with Botticelli

J. Scott Lee
Association for Core Texts and Courses

Using the classical distinction between fine and liberal against mechanical and useful arts, Joshua Reynolds, in his *Discourses on Art*, argues that professional painting can be a liberal art, depending upon the exercise of the mind employed in the practice of the profession (55). For Reynolds, an education which arduously leads from skills, through imitation of the masters, to the fusion of ideas with paint is the royal road to liberal painting: "If deceiving the eye were the only business of art, there is no doubt, indeed, but the minute painter would be more apt to succeed: but it is not the eye, it is the mind, which the painter of genius desires to address" (50). In this instruction, not competence, but genius is the outcome. It is easy to see Reynolds, the aristocrat, as the bearer of outmoded conceptions of art and education that are so elitist that no respectable citizen of a democratic society would wish to employ them. Yet buried within his classical call for disciplinary rigor and real elitism are some quite contemporary notions.

His statement that "it is indisputably evident that a great part of every man's life must be employed in collecting materials for the exercise of genius" may have a certain gender bias, but genius is not confined in that statement to the elite (31). His assertion that "invention in painting does not imply the invention of the subject; for that is commonly supplied by the Poet or Historian" at first seems quite disciplinarily restrictive. But upon second thought, Reynolds is rather explicit that not only must the subjects of the liberal painter be multidisciplinary, but that the culture contains a ready stock of subjects, especially for institutes of learning: "Every seminary of learning may be said to be surrounded with an atmosphere of floating knowledge, where every mind may imbibe somewhat congenial to its own original conceptions" (21). Moreover, he is not only convinced that the mass media of print makes these widely available, and that education enhances that availability, but that there are no universal subjects *per se*, but what the culture seems to make so, precisely through controlling the means of media, education, and art itself: "Strictly speaking," he writes, "no subject can be universal, hardly can it be of general concern; but there are events and characters so popularly known in those countries where our Art is in request, that they may be considered as sufficiently general for all our purposes. Such are the great events of Greek and Roman fable and history, which early education, and the usual course of reading, have made familiar and interesting to all of Europe" (55).

Indeed, sometimes his notion of invention, the ultimate product of genius, seems to be deconstructed to the point where he almost appears to be arguing that the culture writes the art work: "invention, strictly speaking, is little more than a new combination of those images which have been previously gathered and deposited into memory" that are, then, directed toward "the great end of the art [which] is to strike the imagination" (31, 57). Even allowing that the culture Reynolds refers to is upper middle class and aristocratic, it hardly seems he is that far away from our notions of the place of the arts, for in these statements, the arts seem comfortably, expressively docile in the hands of the well-heeled, well-educated, controllers of the means of representation. Maybe the most we could say is that Reynolds seems to have merely missed the boat in a kind of characteristic way. His concern with genius seems to be a displacement toward the private, striking the imagination instead of the established order.

I am intrigued by Reynolds' association of professional education with a liberal mind and his further association of the cultural milieu of the artist with things invented. And I am less concerned with making him seem deconstructionist, which he is not, than I am with the tendency in both modern and ancient classical discussions for cultural, political, or, even, disciplinary ends to subsume art under them, whereas Reynolds seems to hold art in high esteem. Undoubtedly, there are times when art is and properly should be subservient. But when that is so, the mind and culture moves elsewhere to look for what it should properly be about. In higher education, this means that the arts, liberal and fine, will be seen as secondary to more important concerns. It is unlikely that liberal education will ever fail to attend to its traditional concerns: the cultivation of the mind, the history of culture, and the preparation of citizens. It is this breadth that gives liberal education its staying power in the face of the development of expertise of the "minute" sort that characterized both Reynolds's profession and our own academies. But the professional education Reynolds advocates requires knowledge and nearly constant consideration of many other disciplines, plus a habit of reflection upon the ideas derived from them.[1] Indeed, this is what makes his fine art of painting liberal and gives to it its fully developed character. More importantly, Reynolds' treatise calls to mind something too frequently forgotten in today's discussions. We speak of liberal and fine arts and, even, liberal arts and sciences, but not liberal disciplines, liberal sciences, or fine disciplines and fine sciences. The arts, liberal or fine, are central to our conception of liberal education. Strictly, cultivation of the mind, history of culture, and even preparation of citizens are, from the point of view of education, consequences of artistic—not political, cultural, or even single disciplinary—activity. If so, then educators might, like Reynolds' painters who seem to need the liberal arts at the beginning and end of their studies, do well to attend to what makes liberal education distinctively artistic. That seemingly small area of "invention," where something new might arise, appears as the proper place to inquire. Sandro Botticelli's *Adoration of the Magi* (1475) illustrates why educators, if the liberal arts are to thrive, might do best to ponder the ways the arts—liberal and fine— integrate disciplines to build new worlds.

The picture in question is an altarpiece. Ruined Roman columns stand off to the left, but Botticelli's scene is focused on a broken down squared-stone wall, now surrounded and covered by a crude "lean-to" of stakes and thatch. On a rise above the foreground, perhaps a "rock" which most would associate with the Church, this "parapet" frames Joseph and the Virgin Mary, who holds out from her body the baby Jesus. From the star of Bethlehem that casts its rays through the framework of roof stakes upon the Holy Family, the principals of the picture fan downward in an arrangement of all who attend the Savior. Within the frame of such ruins, the eye descends to work its way through an "historical" scene with a strangely modern cast.

The most prominent in this scene is the first Magi who, with his gift of gold in front of him, kneels to kiss the Savior's foot. The likeness is of Cosimo d'Medici, grandfather of a clan of Medici's, all present in this picture. Lower to the right, the two other Magi kneel looking to each other, as they await their turn with their gifts. These are Cosimo's sons. To the left, standing dressed in an extraordinary white toga, is Cosimo's grandson, Lorenzo, "Il Magnifico." To the right across the picture and in front of a crowd, stands his younger brother, Giovanni, dressed in a black jerkin. Over to the far right are two figures. "Up stage" against one part of the stone wall, among many who are looking upon the scene, is one figure who points to himself and looks out to the audience of the painted scene. This is Guasparre del Lama, who having had an entrepreneurial career ascending from the ranks of the laboring class to a money changer, commissioned this altarpiece and who may have requested that Botticelli feature his patrons, the Medici, in its arrangement. To the lower right, mirroring the direction of the gaze if not the countenance of del Lama, is the young, twenty-year old Botticelli, who would have had motive enough to include the Medici.[2]

The entire effect of the ensemble is precisely the same effect produced by any proper arrangement of figures on a raked, proscenium stage so that the audience may see the action. We are invited to focus our attention on and to feel something about the links of family, politics, the public, banking, and art, and to think sensitively about representatives of this entire society witnessing a gesture of humility by the greatest of all leaders toward a god-child and the humblest of women and men. Cosimo's sons look at each other as if to say "who is next after father." Lorenzo gazes upward at his grandfather, Giovanni reflects with eyes cast down, and some witnesses of the scene direct their gaze and gestures toward the older and younger Medici's, as if learning how to kneel from masters. In turn, the humble figures of the Holy Family sit atop a pyramid of representatives of the (masculine) modern social order amidst the ruins of an older culture, the heroic virtues clearly subordinate to the virtue of humility.

Modern figures entering historical scenes happened frequently enough in Renaissance painting so that we wish to make no claim that Botticelli was the first to make this sort of theatrical collapse of history and modernity. But what does interest us here is what art was doing at the time, and we do not mean by "art" simply painting, though such a work represents a "discipline" that was engaged widely in "advancement" of artistic and, therefore, cultural frontiers. We are interested, then, in how art is changing the way people think and see, not how it is merely reflecting thought already "written" in the culture.

The action of the painting would be "historical," that is, accepted by the audience of this picture as true. And, of course, so would the Christian virtue it exhibits, at least in so far as it was aligned with the historical story of the three Magi. The persuasiveness of the picture, the picture's ability to bring one to focus upon it, depends on a construction that at some point calls forth in an audience's observations its recognition of the scene. That "statement" by the picture is, indeed, part of the "writing" of the picture by the culture. But what matters more is that the audience would recognize the collapse of history and modernity through the insertion of living figures into the ancient scene. The Florentines may well have lived near ruins, and the Renaissance—the recovery of the lost world of the ancients—may have been a part of their ongoing discourse, at least among certain circles. But for all that and a familiarity with paintings replete with interpretations of Biblically historical events set into contemporaneous surroundings, there is no reason to think that Florentines and we cannot perceive when we are being asked to observe the collapse of the distinction between the past and the present, between history and art.

One is tempted to say that the contemporaneous figures are all "playing their part" upon the stage and are "assuming their roles" for the sake of the honor of being observed by the public in association with the Epiphany. They appear, in Machiavelli's sense of that word, as pious and, in Cosimo's case, tender. (They are all reverently quiet; none of the participants has his mouth open in speech.) And, indeed, the Medici played an active role in the Compagnia de' Magi, the brotherhood which, a bit like krews planning the New Orleans Mardi Gras, met to plan the Feast of the Epiphany. At the very least, then, certain groups within the Florentine culture seem to "paint" the painting, long before Botticelli picks up his brush, co-opting a Biblical scene for their own aggrandizement. As has been observed, in a scene of "Christian piety" the picture "reflects the destinies and dependent relations of people in the Renaissance city where the ruling bankers [in an ostensibly republican city] were pleased to don the attire of the three kings."[3]

But when we ask, "is this what the Medici would have done were the Baby Jesus available to them," we have entered the world of possibility. We now have a problem of credibility; simply painting figures into a Biblical scene does not make it so any more than enactment in a play or festival does. Yet, the painting fixes the image in a way that the stage spectacle, given its dependence on continuous, yet ephemeral presentation, cannot. We are now "permanently" asked, could this be so?

What is undeniable about the painting is that in synthesizing elements of Biblical history, religious veneration, Roman history, and contemporary leadership, the painting destroys the distinctions between the past and the present.[4] But so, in fact, would the Festival of the Epiphany—another *artistic* event. What difference does it make to the collapse of this distinction between past and present that these are works of art? Certainly whether we look at the production of the single artist or the collective production of the Campagnia, in order for the collapse to take place, to exist, these productions *must be* separated from their material, living authors. Put differently, they must be "completed." Botticelli laid upon his altarpiece his pigments and handed the altarpiece over to del Lama, and went on to paint different pictures in different homes of the well heeled. The leaders of the city planned and executed their festival, handed it over to the public, and went on to concern themselves with the governing of cities, armies, and banks. And this means that the syntheses of past and present, made by Festival or artist, are utterly dependent on art for their coming into being and, in the case of the painting, their continuation.

The synthesis of past and present, of banker, Christ, and observing artist, would not have existed except for the art—be it Festival or painting. The moment of this painting never happened in this particularity and as such, to have re-presented "the Medici" in such an a-historical setting is not only to honor them, but also literally to place the figures of them before and beneath God. Without the separate production of such works, this bowing and adoration by the Medici before any person would not have been *seen* and few would have *contemplated or felt the emotions attendant upon the scene* in any activity by the living participants. Imagine any of the Medici entering into this kind of action without the art. True, we might say that the Christian culture with its exaltation of humility prepared the way for this painting, or we might try to discover an extraordinary set of historical, parallel circumstances that would bring about a similar gesture—indeed, that is what the Magi legend is supposed to have been. But without art—textual and visual—no one sees this inversion of humility and pride, and it is nearly unimaginable. Indeed, quite probably, without textual artifacts separated from the authors who wrote the early Christian gospels, preserving the notion that the kingly[5] are worshipful in an act of adoration, we would be unable to identify Christian culture in this aspect or with this "content." Hence, only if the entire male society from artisan, to money-changer, to patriarch had had the opportunity and the wisdom to adore the Christ, and only if his mother extended that opportunity to them, only then would it be so. And only in art is it so.

The consequence, from a political point of view, is to provide a not-political, not-social, even a not-cultural platform—art—from which we may finally join the audience of the Medici, to whom the painter's image looks out, to "criticize" this political scene. Only by being separated by art from our politics can we ever hope to escape the tyranny of culture. In this picture, we do that, by seeing, not just faintly imagining, what it would take to make our leaders and society—in all their majesty, richness, vanity, enculturated clubiness, and dependent relations—bring themselves to the bar of humility. It would take a supreme leader. Even those who were in his family would have trouble bending their knees. Among the ranks of those aspiring to be noticed and elevated, a leading act of humility would ripple through society as a stone's cast into a pond moves toward the shore. Yet, for anyone truly to be at the bar, the politically connected would all have to be present; it would not do to have the "three kings" bow in a private meeting.[6] Though some witnesses might be so pre-occupied with themselves for having made such a scene possible that they might look out to see its effects on others, not only the connected of society would need to learn from their leaders, but so might any witnessing audience whose eyes are focused by the scene's arrangement. This is a conception devoutly to be wished—one which our democratic yearnings for equality may have slowly worked into our culture over succeeding generations. And, it is a conception which is simply inconceivable without art.

No one discipline will give us the richness of conception that the Renaissance bestowed: not painting, not religious studies, not the history of Roman or Italian culture, nor any textual conception which relies only on the art of encoding what a culture writes. Professionalism is simply not deep enough. But if art is to make a new world for us, instead of merely serving the old, it must use, and welcome, all its resources. So, too, if we are to be liberal of mind. This use of resources confers an autonomy, not a dependence, in a liberal mind, and if we want to defend the liberal arts, we must recognize the stake they have in their autonomy from culture and politics and any given discipline. That autonomy is not one of indifference or ignorance. Rather, it is the recognition that the education of liberal artists is toward enabling them to innovate, to make the world anew—in science, politics, and art. Celebrating the arts, liberal or fine, is not simply an homage to the past. With Botticelli's painting that is almost impossible. Instead, we want our students and ourselves to be looking into the future. That is the value of a liberal mind and a liberal education. Both imagine the possible.

Notes

1. In the context of describing both an academy and a process of education, he speaks constantly of arts that "tend to soften and humanise the mind," (20) that the "value and rank of every art is in proportion to the mental labour employed on it, or the mental pleasure produced by it. As this principle is observed or neglected, our profession becomes either a liberal art, or a mechanical trade" (55), and that "every man whose business is description, ought to be tolerably conversant with the poets, in some language or other . . . [to] enlarge his stock of ideas. He ought to acquire an habit of comparing and digesting his notions. He ought not to be wholly unacquainted with . . . philosophy which gives an insight into human nature, and relates to the manners, characters, passions, and affections. He ought to know *something* about the human mind, as well as *a great* deal concerning the body of man" and, then, of course, Reynolds expects his painters to know their history as well (Discourse VII).
2. The description of the figures and its Biblical scene is owed to Rose-Marie and Rainer Hagen in their *What Great Paintings Say*.
3. Hagen, 81.
4. This is so, even with the Roman ruins, for these would not have been ruins in the time of Jesus, any more than this scene took place in the time of the Medici.
5. Or, following the idea that the original, not the Medici, magi are astrologers—the knowledgeable.
6. As they seem to be in the "historical" gospel (Matthew 2.11).

Works Cited

Hagen, Rose-Marie and Rainer. *What Great Paintings Say.* 2 vols. Koln: Taschen, 2003, 76-81.

Reynolds, Joshua, *Discourses on Art.* London: Collier Books, Collier-Macmillan, 1966.

Culture and Patriarchy: The Egalitarian Vision of Woolf's *Three Guineas*

James Woelfel
University of Kansas

Virginia Woolf's *Three Guineas*, published in 1938, is her most passionate and powerful long essay. Writing as Nazi Germany was accelerating its march to war, she argued for the linkage between male domination of women and social-economic hierarchy, imperialism, fascism, racism, and the glorification of war. With savage wit and extensive documentation she relentlessly exposed the social and cultural dominance of patriarchy in nineteenth- and twentieth-century Britain, and offered a vision of culture—of the intellectual, moral, and artistic values of educated, mostly middle-class Britons—based on what women of intelligence and talent had learned from being subordinated and belittled. My title, "Culture and Patriarchy," is intended to evoke Matthew Arnold's influential 1869 essay *Culture and Anarchy*. In presenting Woolf's approach to culture I will suggest a few illuminating contrasts between the two essays: Arnold's vigorous critique of Victorian society in the light of a vision of culture that was liberal and reformist, keenly aware of class but entirely oblivious to gender; and

Woolf's angry, long-simmering feminist assault on the very foundations of Arnold's vision of culture and all that it implied.

By focusing on Woolf's idea of culture, which she develops the most fully in the third and final chapter of *Three Guineas*, I'm simply passing over her original and provocative reflections on a wide range of issues in this rich and complex book. Among them are her devastating characterization of gender relations and arrangements in the nineteenth and twentieth centuries, her satirical portraits of male rituals and costume, her radical vision of what a university education should be and proposals for reform of the professions, her calling upon the state to pay homemakers for their labor, her telling criticisms of Anglican church leaders for their refusal to ordain women, and of course, her indictment of war and violence and many forms of discrimination as deeply rooted in patriarchy.

Three Guineas, which Woolf conceived as a sequel to *A Room of One's Own*, is in the form of a letter replying to a lawyer who has written her an appeal asking, "How are we to prevent war?" and urging her to sign a letter to the newspapers, join the society he represents, and make a contribution to the society. In the course of her response, Woolf incorporates letters from two other people who have written asking her for financial help: one from the treasurer of a women's college, and another from the honorary treasurer of an organization helping women who are seeking professional employment. Woolf finally decides, after exhaustive analysis of the requests and their implications, to contribute to each of the three organizations one guinea.[1]

In chapter 3, writing as one of the "daughters of educated men," as she calls them, Woolf responds specifically to the lawyer's request that she sign a manifesto pledging the signers "to protect culture and intellectual liberty" (85). She points out that the culture he is talking about is one from which women have been systematically excluded until very recently. She writes that "culture for the great majority of educated men's daughters must still be that which is acquired outside the sacred gates, in public libraries or in private libraries, whose doors by some unaccountable oversight have been left unlocked. It must still, in the year 1938, largely consist in reading and writing in our own tongue" (89). Women can only help men defend the dominant culture run by and for men, which she calls the "paid-for" culture, by defending their own hard-won, "unpaid-for" culture.

Turning to the question of a working definition of "culture and intellectual liberty," Woolf immediately dismisses the lofty definitions of culture set forth by eminent writers of the past such as Matthew Arnold, since their definitions apply only to "paid-for" or patriarchal culture (90). Arnold had defined culture as "the study of perfection" (409),[2] the pursuit of the ideal—of "the best that has been thought and known in the world" —in every aspect of life: intellectual, artistic, moral, political, religious. "[W]hat distinguishes culture," he wrote, "is, that it is possessed by the scientific passion as well as by the passion of doing good; that it demands worthy notions of reason and the will of God, and does not readily suffer its own crude conceptions to substitute themselves for them" (410). Culture is the inner cultivation of the uniquely *"humane* spirit" that elevates us above "animality," a cultivation that leads us to evaluate human beings individually and corporately in terms of their "best self" rather than their "everyday self" (422, 443, 453). Arnold spent much of *Culture and Anarchy* criticizing the "Philistinism" and hyper-individualism of English attitudes in religion, commerce, and politics, and exposing the narrowness and particularism of outlook of each of the three great class divisions. Culture, he argued, imbues us with a disinterested vision of our common humanity and best selves that can bring us together across class, religious, and political differences, break down our hyper-individualism in favor of a commitment to the common good, and effect a gradual ennobling and equalizing revolution in the life of society. Culture, Arnold wrote, "Seeks to do away with classes," and "men of culture" are "the true apostles of equality" (426-427).

Speaking for the "unpaid-for" culture of women, Woolf offers a very modest and "crude" definition of culture as "the disinterested pursuit of reading and writing the English language," and of intellectual liberty as "the right to say or write what you think in your own words, and in your own way" (91). The key term for Woolf is "disinterested," since male advocates of culture like Arnold have set so much store by the ability to rise above differences of class, religion, and politics (with differences of gender of course unmentioned) as the hallmark of the man of culture. Woolf argues that women writers and readers can practice the disinterestedness that belongs to culture only by, first, becoming economically independent—a goal which in 1938 many were still struggling to achieve against formidable obstacles; and, second, by the committed and austere pursuit of truth both personally and publicly and the refusal to compromise their integrity to the blandishments of money, charm, and publicity. "To protect culture and intellectual liberty in practice would mean," she writes, ". . . ridicule and chastity, loss of publicity and poverty. But those . . . are . . . [women's] familiar teachers" (100).

Earlier in *Three Guineas* Woolf has spelled out what she means by these "familiar teachers": virtues she believes women should have acquired through their history of subordination and exclusion: 1) the first is *poverty*, which as a virtue (rather than an imposed condition) means simply "enough money to live upon," to enable one to be independent; 2) the second virtue is *chastity*: "when you have made enough to live on by your profession you must refuse to sell your brain for the sake of money"—a prostitution worse than prostitution of the body; 3) derision, the third of women's "familiar teachers," means that "you must refuse all methods of advertising merit, and hold that ridicule, obscurity, and censure are preferable, for psychological reasons, to fame and praise"; and 4) The last of the virtues women should have learned is *"freedom from unreal loyalties"*—"you must," says Woolf, "rid yourself of pride of nationality . . . of religious pride, college pride, school pride, family pride, sex pride and those unreal loyalties that spring from them" (80).

Having had these teachers, Woolf suggests to her correspondent, women "should be able to take a more purely disinterested view of culture than their brothers, without for a moment claiming . . . that they are by nature more disinterested" (100). On the basis of their historical and continuing experience as objects of discrimination and exclusion, women should have a greater capacity than men to take a disinterested—that is, a detached and actively critical—attitude toward the reigning patriarchal culture. It is a culture defined by materialism and commercialism, entrenched hierarchy and class exploitation, a patriotism based on imperialism and racism, and the accompanying institutionalization of violence and war; and underpinning them all, what Woolf calls "unreal loyalties"—illusory and idolatrous attachments to these oppressive social and cultural arrangements.

In one of the most powerful passages in *Three Guineas*, Woolf makes the case to her correspondent for the indissoluble link between nineteenth-century women's battle for equal rights and opportunities and the contemporary struggle against fascism and its victims: "They were fighting the tyranny of the patriarchal state as you are fighting the tyranny of the Fascist state. Thus we are merely carrying on the same fight that our mothers and grandmothers fought" (102). Woolf believes that the rise of Italian, German, and Spanish fascism has simply exposed, in its extreme form, the "monster" of inequality and oppression that pervades British society and human society generally. This monster, she tells her correspondent,

> is making distinctions not merely between the sexes, but between the races. . . . Now you are being shut out, you are being shut up, because you are Jews, because you are democrats, because of race, because of religion. . . . The whole iniquity of dictatorship, whether in Oxford or Cambridge, in Whitehall or Downing Street, against Jews or against women, in England, or in Germany, in Italy or in Spain is now apparent to you. (102-3)

Here, not quite seventy years after Matthew Arnold's genteel appeal to culture as a social ennobler and equalizer and to "men of culture" as "the true apostles of equality," we have a more radically egalitarian vision of the function of "culture." Arnold could still ignore completely the protests against gender inequity that were being raised even in his day, and could frame his theory of culture in a nation that felt powerful, stable, and optimistic. To Woolf, writing in 1938, neither of those assumptions was credible.

While the "daughters of educated men" share a common humanity and a common struggle for peace and justice with "educated men" such as her correspondent, Woolf concludes that women like her can help the most effectively to promote culture and protect individual rights by refusing to join societies such as his and instead forming an "Outsiders' Society." "It would consist," she writes, "of educated men's daughters working in their own class . . . and by their own methods for liberty, equality, and peace" (106). Once again, the reason is that women have been excluded from the dominant culture and, now that they are finally permitted the opportunity for an education and a job, are in danger of being co-opted by ideals and assumptions which they, as "outsiders," do not and ought not share. The practice of the four "virtues" of poverty, chastity, derision, and freedom from unreal loyalties engenders an alternative critical perspective that will have the healthy effect of challenging the prevailing conventions on patriotism, human rights, national and personal security, economics, education, and religion—conventions which even liberal-minded men often uncritically share.

Three Guineas is a subtle and complex book, its arguments somewhat undigested and inconsistent, but it is also a powerful and disturbing feminist statement worthy to stand alongside Beauvoir's *The Second Sex*. Sixty-five years after its publication, Woolf's call for a fundamental revaluation of the meaning of culture in the light of the demand for inclusiveness and equality still challenges us and our students as we continue to struggle toward a far-from-realized goal.

Notes

1. One pound one shilling or twenty-one shillings; not actually coined after 1813, but widely used in pricing professional fees, subscriptions to societies and institutions, works of art and other luxury items, and sometimes landed property, until the British converted to a decimal coinage system in the 1970s.
2. Woolf's father, Leslie Stephen, like Arnold an eminent Victorian, knew Arnold and loved his poetry, above all his poem "The Scholar Gypsy." (Woolf herself was only six when Arnold died.) Interestingly, in an essay in America's *Vogue* magazine in 1924, Woolf included Arnold among writers who "are not men when they write, nor are they women. They appeal to that large tract of the soul which is sexless" (462). We are reminded here of Woolf's admiration for Shakespeare and Jane Austen in *A Room of One's Own* because in their writings they manage to transcend gender identification and special pleading and achieve a kind of "androgyny." However, Arnold as a Victorian essayist and public figure would certainly not have escaped Woolf's withering attack on patriarchal culture in modern Britain.

Works Cited

Arnold, Matthew. "Culture and Anarchy." *Poetry and Criticism of Matthew Arnold.* Ed. A. Dwight Culler. Boston: Houghton Mifflin, 1961.

Woolf, Virginia. *Three Guineas.* New York: Harcourt Brace Jovanovich, 1966.

---. *The Essays of Virginia Woolf.* Ed. Andrew McNeillie. Vol. 3. San Diego: Harcourt Brace Jovanovich, 1988.

Spoken from the Heart: Apprehending the Passion of Harriet Beecher Stowe

Elizabeth Dell
Baylor University

In 1850, enraged by the passing of the Fugitive Slave Law and sorrowing over the loss of her infant son to cholera, Harriet Beecher Stowe felt a "mighty wind" rush through her, the result of which was *Uncle Tom's Cabin, or Life Among the Lowly* (1851-52), the novel that aroused the emotions of a nation. Her work remains one of the most, if not the most, politically passionate works within the American canon; indeed, it endured neglect and even ridicule as a literary work because of its overemphasis on pathos and sentiment until Jane Tompkins resurrected it in 1985. In the past two decades, *Uncle Tom's Cabin* has enjoyed considerable attention; many critics have celebrated it as the defining (white) woman's novel of the nineteenth century, and around it a large body of criticism has arisen. Among many arguments is the discussion over her use of pathos—whether finally it is liberating or containing—whether its purpose in moving readers to feel the power of liberal democracy finally is eroded through its idealization of white middle-class values. Regardless of one's point of view, the novel affords a tremendous opportunity pedagogically for those of us who teach in core text programs to produce "communities and cultures of learning." Even as her ideology of equality based on romantic racialism and even domestic womanhood seems dated, Stowe's passion for social justice and for drama engages students.

There is so much that is teachable in the novel about American culture in the nineteenth century, from issues of race, class, and gender to the role of religion and the conflict between sectionalism and nationalism, that it is hard to know where to begin. For the course that can devote a considerable chunk of time to *Uncle Tom's Cabin* (and unfortunately this may be a luxury one cannot afford), focusing on several readings from the Age of Reform can illuminate many of these rich areas. Ideally, a smattering of readings would be best: Ralph Waldo Emerson and Henry David Thoreau to examine the Transcendentalist's focus on conscience and political activism, Jonathan Edwards to consider the importance of religious revivalism and the rise of Protestant evangelicalism, Elizabeth Cady Stanton and Margaret Fuller to highlight the movement for women's equality, and Frederick Douglass and Harriet Jacobs to stress the powerful effect of slave narratives on the antislavery movement. And perhaps something on territorial expansion, Jacksonian democracy, and early industrialism would be valuable as well. But once the underpinnings of American culture (social, political, historical, economic) have been established, where should one go from there?

I suggest that one begins with the passion—the passion that incited Stowe to write this novel. The tragedy of human bondage struck a very real chord in this middle-class Northern wife and mother of a half dozen children, who, by all accounts, knew little personally about the slave experience. Students might be asked to think subjectively, for a moment, about Stowe's personal identification with largely imagined oppressed peoples and to consider how that identification led her to create her work of fiction. A letter that Stowe wrote to an admirer in December of 1852, shortly after completing her novel, might provide a starting point. She responds to Eliza Cabot Follen, an abolitionist and fellow writer whose published work of nursery verse Stowe has read to her own children; no doubt, these multiple connections spur Stowe to reply from the heart, one woman of similar experience to another. Giving a brief and comical account of her appearance—"somewhat more than forty, about as thin and dry as a pinch of snuff" (Stowe 172)—Stowe describes a less-than-romantic marriage to the clergyman Calvin Stowe: "a man rich in Greek and Hebrew and Latin and Arabic, and alas, rich in nothing else" (Stowe 172); the quick succession of seven births that both physically and mentally depleted her; the effect of her fifth child's death: "It was at his dying bed and at his grave that I learned what a poor slave mother may feel when her child is torn away from her" (Stowe 173); and the years of poverty and hard work: "The nursery and the kitchen were my principal fields of labor" (Stowe 173) that drove her to write so that she might purchase a "feather bed!" (Stowe 173).

Students benefit from a brief discussion of women's, including white middle-class women's, role in the nineteenth century—the exhaustion from child-birthing and the sorrow of losing so many loved ones to various untreatable diseases. These were fairly universal, but class and race—the extraordinary poverty of the new immigrants, for example, and the agony of slavery—provided further complications and sorrows for women. This last pained Stowe, and to Follen she expresses "exquisite suffering":

> This horror, this nightmare abomination! Can it be in my country! It lies like lead on my heart, it shadows my life with sorrow; the more so that I feel, as for my own brothers, for the South, and am pained by every horror I am obliged to write, as one who is forced by some awful oath to disclose in court some family disgrace. (Stowe 177)

Writing with her "heart's blood," Stowe makes clear her sympathy for the slave. Much of this passion stems from her identification with woman's primary role as nurturer, a predominant view in the nineteenth century. Because a woman's heart better apprehends another's sorrow—because woman is an emotional creature and because sentiment holds a purer path to Christian truths—it falls upon white women to be the moral arbiter and to persuade their male kin to right the wrong of slavery.

Thus, students also need sufficient background to comprehend Stowe's evangelicalism, which is so much the source of her passion. Indeed, passion, in Uncle Tom's Cabin, comes to mean that of Christ, and a number of scholars, including Tompkins and Elizabeth Ammons, liken the twinned stories of Little Eva and Uncle Tom to the sufferings of Christian martyrs. At a Christian institution of higher learning, one can be bold about these connections, and mostly students "get it," although that may draw some of them away from the focus on the textual specifics toward their own paths to redemption. At a secular institution, such a reading, though possibly tricky, can be contextualized within the historical and cultural tradition of which Stowe, all her of family, and much of the nation were so much a part. Nineteenth-century Americans did not need footnotes to read Stowe's transparent connection between Hagar the elderly slave woman in chapter 12, "Select Incident of Lawful Trade," who is sold away from her remaining son, and the Old Testament story of the surrogate mother and slave who bore a child by Abraham: Ishmael, who supposedly fathered the line of nomadic Bedouins; nor would these Americans have overlooked the passages in the same chapter that refer to the Sermon on the Mount. In short, students might want to investigate the power of Stowe's argument against slavery and consider why it overtly turns to the Christian tradition rather than to the language of the Founding Fathers. Why did the Bible hold greater sway with Stowe's audience than the Constitution? And with any luck some bright student will recall the dilemma with which the delegates to the Philadelphia convention faced the issue of slavery and the unfinished work of that document in regard to slavery and will make the connection that the Christian story of salvation held greater truths for the majority of nineteenth-century Americans than the Constitution, still only a half-century old.

Such a discussion may prompt students to think about the kinds of arguments made today and about such hot topics as abortion and the death penalty (and where one takes these discussions would depend on both the nature of the particular class, including its identity, and of the institution.) Depending on student interest and the direction of the course, one might mention Martin Luther King, Jr.'s celebrated *Letter from Birmingham Jail* (1963) in which, a man of the cloth himself, he addresses the concerns of both pastors and rabbis who have accused him and the SCLC of being both "unwise" and "untimely" (King). One hundred years later, after the publication of *Uncle Tom's Cabin*, King feels compelled to speak to all monotheistic traditions (Christian, Judean and Islamic), calling upon each to recall the relation of their faith to just law and individual conscience. In a century, then, this great civil rights leader bases his arguments on the Constitution and on a definition of justice that seeks a universal truth common to all three religions. For a segment of Americans, the Christian story still resonates and calls citizens to action. (Witness the recent phenomenon of The Passion of the Christ and the reports of murderers, overpowered by this film, repenting of their crimes). But for many Americans the unfinished debate that began in 1787 of equality for all is now answered solely by the Constitution and the laws of the land. Stowe's dependence on the Christian story might be historically and aesthetically interesting but not moving in and of itself and perhaps alien and discomforting. Even so, students can be shown that *Uncle Tom's Cabin* is admirable for its insistence that the nation could extend the status of citizen to the African American. With her "heart's blood," Stowe moved many mid-century Americans and participated in a great struggle to redefine what it is to be a human being.

Works Cited

King, Martin Luther. Letter from a Birmingham Jail. New York. Harper Collins, 1994.

Stowe, Harriet Beecher. *Life and Letters of Harriet Beecher Stowe.* Ed. Annie Fields. Boston: Houghton and Mifflin, 1897.

---. *Uncle Tom's Cabin.* Intro. Amanda Claybaugh. New York: Barnes and Noble Classics, 2003.

Constructing and Deconstructing the *Gospel of John*

Lillian I. Larsen
Columbia University

Whether focusing on the importance of a text to the literary historical tradition, or on its significance to contemporary culture, the Literature Humanities arm of the Columbia University Core names its objective as one of "considering particular conceptions of what it means to be human and the place of such conceptions in the development of critical thought."[1] The *Gospel of John*, routinely distinguished as the 'most spiritual' of the four canonical gospels, might easily be regarded as a minefield of religious invective working against such an egalitarian agenda. Peppered with language and imagery that pictures the nascent Christian movement as grossly misunderstood and beleaguered by the religious establishment of its day, this apology for "us" against "them" has historically been dangerously persuasive, and pervasive, in fueling a highly dualistic, sectarian worldview and even legitimating violence.[2] To echo the hyperbole of the gospel itself: Were every [ideological exposition of this text] to be published, one might suppose that world itself could not contain the books (John 21:25). In contrast, a very small library would be quite adequate for housing the few exemplars of disinterested elucidation.[3]

On one level, it is a measure of the persuasive effect of this intensely valued and theologically laden narrative that little attention has historically been paid its classical and Jewish literary antecedents. With regard to classical precedents, in particular, long-standing, if arbitrary, dichotomies have colored even the most routine efforts at contextualization. A polemic against asserting "pagan" influence on the textual traditions of Early Christianity is articulated as far back as Tertullian's second-century query, "What has Athens to do with Jerusalem?" In a contemporary frame, New Testament scholar Abraham Malherbe posits that Tertullian's concern in maintaining the distinctiveness of Christian faith is not far removed from that of more recent readers, "convinced that the authority of the New Testament would be weakened if it could be demonstrated that its 'essential beliefs' were derived from a pagan [or secular] milieu" (Malherbe 1).

While much of the conversation around the "true" reading of the *Gospel of John* has quite legitimately centered on questions of Jewish Christian relations, few discussions move beyond this to the rich literary discourse that characterizes the narrative itself. Yet it is only when reading this gospel within its classical and Jewish frame that we begin to appreciate the manner in which the final redactor has liberally availed himself of stock characters and structures from each tradition. Given an audience comprised of Hellenized Jews and "god-fearing" gentiles, such an interweaving of the storied traditions of Hebrew Scripture and the classical "canon" is hardly surprising. Writing at a point when the rift between the nascent Christian movement and its Rabbinic counterpart had become definitive,[4] the *Johannine* redactor leaves no literary stone unturned in framing his hero in familiar and sympathetic terms.

Here the conflicts between Moses and the Pharaoh, Dionysus and Pentheus, have been masterfully conflated and re-envisioned in a vivid and compelling portrayal of the stand-off between Jesus and the Jewish religio-political establishment of his day. Recurring "I am" statements,[5] the seven *semeia*, or signs, that structure the early part of the text,[6] and an extended Passover "symposium" echo and invert the Exodus story. Water turned into wine, a chorus of female initiates, and the costumed drama of the Passion, underscore a *Bacchic* subplot in this altercation between established authority and a charismatic, divinely inspired upstart.

To a thoroughly Hellenized, first-century audience, and the Literature Humanities student newly steeped in classical narrative and Hebrew scripture, Jesus' turning of water into an abundance of fine wine at a local wedding melds the imagery attached to the epiphany of the god at the feast of Dionysus, (Euripides 142-43) with its Rabbinic counterpart, the abundance of wine at the wedding banquet that will herald the days of the Messiah.[7] John's likening of Jesus to the *logos* in the prologue of the gospel immediately calls up not only the physically creative "word" of Genesis but also the intellectually creative *logos* of Plato's *Symposium*.

Sophisticated forensic rhetoric invites the audience, and inadvertently the reader, to arbitrate the testimony of an ever-widening circle of witnesses. These attestations frame an *agov* that begins with the early corroboration of John the Baptist (John 1:19-34) and culminates in the final begrudging admissions of "doubting Thomas" (John 20:24-29). All claim Jesus as an immortal, messianic figure in the face of stubborn opposition to such assertions.[8] Miraculous signs provide material evidence. These mimic, and inadvertently trump, the series of wonders that Moses performed to convince the Egyptian Pharaoh of the legitimacy of his message in the days preceding the Jewish Exodus.

Consistent with the comic hyperbole that characterizes the Exodus account, and the juxtaposition of comedy and tragedy in the *Bacchae*, *John*'s redactor exercises full poetic license in weaving together this series of increasingly exaggerated *semeia*.[9] Interspersed with more widely attributed miracle stories, the most dramatic of the "signs" appear only in this gospel. At the wedding feast referenced above, Jesus not only turns water into wine; he produces circa one hundred and fifty gallons of quality vintage (John 2:1-11). At the pool of Bethesda, Jesus does not heal some garden-variety sick man, but one who has been "ill for thirty-eight years" (John 5:1-8). In the temple on the Sabbath, Jesus does not simply restore sight to a blind man, but to one who was "blind from . . . birth" (John 9:1-7). In the raising of Lazarus, Jesus does not merely resurrect a man who is dead; he resurrects a man who has been "in the tomb for four days" (John 11:1-44).[10] In a well-executed melding of comedy and tragedy, the hyperbole of this seventh *semeion* serves not only to signal the apex of Jesus' power and popular appeal. It also marks his *peripateia*, as it becomes the impetus for the tragic reversal that will lead to his demise.

Further parallels could be drawn, but these will suffice to make my point. It is only by contextualizing religious prose within a broad narrative tradition, that the very human enterprise of constructing religious "truth" can finally be elucidated and the persuasive force of religious imagery critically engaged. If we accept that "all literature can only develop within, and out of, a distinct historical and intellectual milieu" (Smith 43), resituating this text within its logical literary trajectory transforms a sectarian minefield into a veritable gold mine for teaching the reading of religious text as "text" rather than creed. In fact, a contextualized analysis of the "us" against "them" dichotomy that characterizes this mythical reconstruction not only demystifies its sectarian rhetoric, it also brings a new appreciation of the persuasive capacity inherent to literary re-imagination and re-invention.

While it is clear that cultivating a critical appreciation of the very human sources of religious rhetoric is vital to the study of religion, I would argue that fostering critical awareness of the constructed nature of religious language and imagery is equally important in the study of literature and the arts. In our current political climate, the importance of equipping students with the analytical expertise to recognize the source, and assess the effect, of rhetoric in which a religiously influenced worldview is operative cannot be overemphasized. A long and easy reliance on the ostensible demarcation between "church and state" has effectively inoculated a large swath of the populace against perceiving and analyzing the import of religiously loaded political prose. In this alternate sphere, religious imagery, albeit potent, is relatively malleable, bearing little or no fixed historical or cultural valence.

If our objective as Core instructors is, indeed, one of "considering particular conceptions of what it means to be human, and the place of such conceptions in the development of critical thought,"[11] in troubling the waters of the comfortable zone where potent religious imagery is routinely employed but its validity rarely interrogated, reading the *Gospel of John* in the Literature Humanities classroom affords a rich context for exploring the ways in which religious prose is imbedded in and informed by culture even as it simultaneously functions to affect and shape culture. Whether this narrative held convincing sway over its original audience remains an open question. Its persuasive effect over two thousand years of ensuing history is clear. In supplying a ready interface between two worlds that have for too long been regarded as ideologically disparate, reading the *Gospel of John* in the Literature Humanities classroom unexpectedly affords a context in which Tertullian's rhetorical question can literally be addressed and the intersection of "Athens" and "Jerusalem" in early Christian textual traditions can be recognized and elucidated.

Notes

1. *Columbia University Literature Humanities Home Page*. Department of the Core Curriculum, Columbia University.
   <http://www.college.columbia.edu/core/classes/lh.php>.
2. I am deeply indebted to Kathy Eden, Professor of Comparative Literature at Columbia University in New York City, and Vincent Wimbush, Professor of Religion at Claremont Graduate University in California, for the interpretive ground in which my treatment of this text is rooted.
3. Ernst Haenchen presents a useful overview of both ancient and modern readings of this text in the introduction to his two volume critical commentary on the Gospel of John.
4. Reference to exclusion from the synagogue within the text of this treatise has led many scholars to postulate this redactor's "us" against "them" dichotomy as a poignant response to just such an occasion. E.g. John 9:18-23.
5. See John 6:35; 8:12; 10:7-9, 11-14; 11:25; 14:6; 15:1; 18:4-6.
6. See John 4:46-54; 5:1-9; 6:1-14; 6:16-21; 9:1-7; 11:1-44; 20:1-10.
7. *Midrash Rabbah* 15.30 on Exodus 12:2.

8. This is marked rhetorically by a progression of widening circles of belief. Following the attestation of John the Baptist in chapter 1, the "signs" begin with Jesus being recognized by those who are most intimate with him: His mother already knows (John 2:5); disciples believe (2:11); many in Jerusalem believe (2:23); many in Samaria believe (4:39); a Roman official believes (4:53); a lame man is healed on the Sabbath (5:9); persecution begins (5:18).
9. Thanks to colleague Rosamund Rodman for calling attention to the escalating hyperbole of these signs.
10. Here we encounter further literary layering as the redactor frames the "unbelief of the Jews" (John 12:37) as a pun on the story unique to the *Gospel of Luke* of one "Lazarus" who died and was afforded residence in Abraham's bosom. The Lukan story ends with the assertion that even if someone were to "rise from the dead" the Jews would not believe (Luke 16:19-31).
11. See *Literature Humanities Home Page.* Columbia University <http://www.college.columbia.edu/core/classes/lh.php>.

Works Cited

Euripides. *The Bacchae and Other Plays.* Trans. Philip Vellacott. Baltimore: Penguin, 1961.

Haenchen, Ernst. *A Commentary on the Gospel of John.* Hermeneia Series. Trans. Robert W. Funk. Vol. I. Philadelphia: Fortress Press, 1984.

Malherbe, Abraham. *Paul and the Popular Philosophers.* Minneapolis: Fortress Press, 1989.

Smith, Jonathan Z. *Drudgery Divine.* Chicago: U of Chicago P, 1990.

Building Communities:
Possibilities and Problems

The "Mythical Method" as a Means to Community in Eliot's *Murder in the Cathedral*

Celia S. Clay
University of Dallas

To have a community requires memory. But the road from the past to the present is not often linear, and for most students today, it almost never is. Still, we marvel that that road can be found, and in surprising places. Imagine, for instance, the following scenario: in the midst of a savory buffet-style undergraduate education, a student is fortunate enough to encounter a work such as *Murder in the Cathedral*, and a recognition of sorts occurs, perhaps the stirrings of memory in a wintry season. The stark, stylized language of the chorus is unlike most of the modern literature he has read, for the words themselves are not ends, and the characters that speak them not personalities, but rough outlines pointing to something else. The effect is almost like looking at an icon, not a mirror, but a window to another reality. He misses the allusions but still recognizes something strange, something "other" in the drama. Later, the student encounters Greek tragedy, and the chorus of Aeschylus strikes him as an oddly familiar voice; in Eliot's chorus, with its contentment in mediocrity, its desire to avoid the "disturbance of the quiet seasons" and not draw attention to itself, could be heard the echo of Aeschylus'. The past and present thus become connected, not only in one's own mind, but also in the consciousness of an entire civilization.

The Greek voice is one among many to be heard in *Murder in the Cathedral*. And it is the polyphonic quality of the drama that leads one to think of it as an example of Eliot's own practice of the "mythical method," which he admires Joyce for employing as a novelist. Joyce's technique, writes Eliot, "is simply a way of controlling, of ordering, of giving a shape and a significance to the immense panorama of futility and anarchy which is contemporary history" (*'Ulysses,' Order, and Myth* 177). Joyce stirs the memory of his reader through allusion: his Ulysses is modern, while it runs on a parallel track with Homer's. Similarly, *Murder in the Cathedral* uses the method of allusion, while maintaining its particular historical moment, the twelfth-century martyrdom of Thomas Becket at Canterbury. Eliot layers modern rationalist history over the medieval morality play, over Greek tragedy, to construct his drama. It contains *Everyman*'s Four Tempters and ends in the canonization of a saint; but present also are the pusillanimous Greek chorus and a prideful protagonist, as well as Four Knights who sound like good old modern Englishmen. The Four Knights are not only Becket's assassins but also his strongest critics, voicing the common modern opinion that the martyr was in fact "overweeningly arrogant," as Grover Smith reminds us (183).

Though its action stays squarely in the twelfth century, allusions to modern rationalism abound in the play. The Fourth Tempter, for example, tells Becket that Thomas's "jeweled shrine" will be destroyed over time, and his miracles discounted by historical fact. And when the Four Knights turn to the audience to defend the killing, past and present intersect as the martyrdom is put on trial before the present day audience. As David Jones observes, the scene could be said to be the temptation of the audience to discount a supernatural event from the perspective of secular reason (62). We are tempted to declare Becket a fanatic of unsound mind, as he warns us we will be. With the defense of the Four Knights, Eliot takes the mythical method a step further than Joyce, by showing that allusion is atemporal not only in the sense of extending into the past, as Joyce's *Ulysses* does, but also in the sense of looking at the things to come. The action of the play contains both past and future: a medieval moment can remember the Greeks and foresee modernity.

This layering of time periods through allusion, Joseph Frank argues in *Spatial Form in Modern Literature*, Eliot constructs so that his readers may "apprehend [his] work spatially, in a moment in time, rather than as a sequence" (9). Frank reminds us that

> For Eliot, the distinctive quality of a poetic sensibility is its capacity to form new wholes, to fuse seemingly disparate experiences into an organic unity. The ordinary man, Eliot writes, 'falls in love or reads Spinoza, and these two experiences have nothing to do with each other, or with the noise of the typewriter or the smell of cooking; in the mind of the poet these experiences are always forming new wholes.'" (10)

Murder in the Cathedral is an illustration of this spatial reality: it holds the Greek, Medieval, and Modern Rationalist perspectives in union in the same moment. And the result of this mythical method, the juxtaposition of the ancient and modern, is that strange iconic quality that leads some to find the characters of the play uncompelling, underdeveloped, devoid of personality.

But perhaps what the stylized characters lack is actually realism. In a time when drama had gotten to the point of carefully setting a dinner table for a dinner scene, Eliot wanted to move away from realism. This move from realism in art, argues Frank, signals that humanity is now out of place in the cosmos, out of harmony with nature as a result of his attempts to conquer it. Frank cites the art historian Wilhelm Worringer's study on the vacillation in art between naturalistic and non-naturalistic styles:

> Naturalism, Worringer points out, always has been created by cultures that have achieved an equilibrium between man and the cosmos . . . . On the other hand, when the relationship between man and the cosmos is one of disharmony and disequilibrium, we find that nonorganic, linear-geometric styles are always produced . . . . Non-naturalistic styles like Byzantine and Romanesque are produced during periods dominated by a religion that rejects the natural world as a realm of evil and imperfection. Instead of depicting the profuse vitality of nature with all its temptations, the will-to-art turns toward spiritualization; it eliminates mass and corporeality and tries to approximate the eternal, ethereal tranquility of otherworldly existence. (53-54)

Eliot's poetry certainly speaks of both ways, spiritualization and earthy vitality: in his *Four Quartets* he describes the "way of vacancy," which is the "desiccation of the world of sense," and the way of "plenitude"—a way that would increase that "profuse vitality of nature" Frank describes ("Burnt Norton" 178-179). But the preoccupation of most of Eliot's poetry is vertical rather than horizontal, a spiritual ascent from the earth in search of the "shaft of sunlight" that the chorus of *Murder in the Cathedral* discovers.

The "shaft of sunlight" in Eliot's play is the hint of a mystical realm that modernity has largely neutralized, in the words of his contemporary, I.A. Richards. Gone is the Magical View of nature, "the belief in a world of Spirits and Powers which control events, and which can be evoked and, to some extent, controlled themselves by human practices." Nature in modernity has been neutralized as a result of the transference from the Magical View of the world to the Scientific. (*Science and Poetry* 515). Indeed, the task of the chorus of *Murder in the Cathedral* is to see themselves once again in harmony with nature, to find the pattern, the order—the wheel and their place on it. But to do this requires first that the Women of Canterbury see themselves in relation to the divine, in a "shaft of sunlight," to see the reality of which mankind cannot bear very much. To attempt this vision is the occupation of the saint, Eliot tells us in "The Dry Salvages," available to most of us only in the moment in the smoky chapel, the moment outside of time. But he asks us to *consider* the transcendent in *Murder in the Cathedral*. And included in the "mythical method" of allusion is this vertical dimension. To allude to the Greeks is to bring in the Greek cosmos, from Olympus to Hades, and to allude to the Medievals is to bring in an ordered nature that harmoniously reflects a designer. If I may allude to an earlier talk by Paul Woodruff, it is to draw in reverence. And reverence implies a community, living and dead, with duties to the divine and the human.

Yet, if one considers the dominant subject matter of Eliot's poems—and verse plays—it might seem strange to speak of them in terms of community, in the flesh and blood, as distinct from the mystical understanding of a community of souls. Eliot's poetry is generally ascetic in sensibility; his setting is desert, and his action often centers on a renunciation of this world. "This is cactus land, this is the dead land," he tells us in "The Hollow Men." The "Fire Sermon" of "The Waste Land" teaches the rejection of passions that the characters in the poem are too apathetic to experience. "April is the cruelest month," because it causes the painful disturbance of the quiet seasons as new life begins to grow beneath the frozen earth. *Murder in the Cathedral* shares the ascetic quality of the poems. Its chorus, composed of the Women of Canterbury, sits in the dead of winter, fearing the disturbance of new life that spring brings. The action of the play is renunciation—martyrdom—the sacrifice of the life of a man for a larger community of souls. And this action takes the chorus along with it into death, and subsequent resurrection. The blood of the martyrs enriches the earth, we are told (part II 84).

It seems that only at the end of the play does the horizon against which the martyrdom has occurred become visible. Only lastly are we given a hint of the horizontal dimension, that "way of plenitude," also known as the way of affirmation, a community opening up in which nature and man exist in accord. The chorus addresses their Creator: "all things affirm thee in living; ... Even in us the voice of seasons, the snuffle of winter, the song of spring, the drone of summer, the voices of beasts and of birds, praise Thee" (part II 84). But this way of affirmation is only possible because of the sacrifices of some: "For the blood of Thy martyrs and Saints shall enrich the earth . . ." (84). The way of "vacancy," the loss of their priest and pastor, has brought the chorus to this point of increase.

As we think about building and rebuilding community, we might wonder, what is the relationship between "vacancy" and "plenitude," to use Eliot's terms, between sacrifice, a renunciation of the world for a higher ideal not present in it, and receptivity, an acceptance and embrace of the world as gift? Reflecting on these two ways as they surface in Eliot's works, one meets the image of ascetic renunciation most often. But also present is the way of affirmation. What, then, is the place of plenitude in Eliot's work? It seems that Eliot moves toward a greater emphasis on community and affirmation, as opposed to renunciation and negation, through his turn to the medium of drama.

In Eliot's plays the ideas of his poetry are perhaps less subtly, at times less beautifully, conveyed, but there is the presence of a new possibility: through dramatized verse, ideas become incarnate on a stage and move horizontally into the world. Eliot reminds us that verse which is audible, visible, in action on a stage, brings poetry to the common man in a way that giving him a volume of poetry to read alone will not. He writes that:

What we have to do is to bring poetry into the world in which the audience lives and to which it returns when it leaves the theatre; not to transport the audience into some imaginary world totally unlike its own, an unreal world in which poetry is tolerated. What I should hope might be achieved, by a generation of dramatists having the benefit of our experience, is that the audience should find, at the moment of awareness that it is hearing poetry, that it is saying to itself, 'I could talk in poetry, too!' Then we should not be transported into an artificial world; on the contrary, our own sordid, dreary daily world would be suddenly illuminated and transfigured." (*Poetry and Drama* 141)

If a sense of community is to be established in our classrooms and our culture revitalized, then teachers, too, as well as dramatists, will have to make of their arenas "imaginary worlds" where past and present come together and poetry is never "tolerated."

Works Cited

Eliot, T.S. *Murder in the Cathedral*. New York: Harcourt, Brace & Company, 1935.

---. *Collected Poems 1909-1962*. New York: Harcourt Brace Jovanovich, 1963.

---. "'Ulysses', Order, and Myth." *Selected Prose of T.S. Eliot*. Ed. Kermode, Frank. New York: Harcourt Brace & Company, 1975.

---. "Poetry and Drama." *Selected Prose of T.S. Eliot*. Ed. Kermode, Frank. New York: Harcourt Brace & Company, 1975.

Frank, Joseph. "Spatial Form in Modern Literature." *The Widening Gyre: Crisis and Mastery in Modern Literature*. New Brunswick, New Jersey: Rutgers UP, 1963.

Jones, David. *The Plays of T.S. Eliot*. Toronto: U of Toronto P, 1960.

Richards, I.A. "Science and Poetry." *Criticism: The Foundations of Modern Literary Judgement*. Ed. Mark Schorer, Josephine Miles, and Gordon McKenzie. New York: Harcourt, Brace & World, 1958.

Smith, Grover. *T.S. Eliot's Poetry and Plays*. Chicago: U of Chicago P, 1956.

Captain Vere,
Liberal Learning, and Leadership

Daniel G. Lang
Lynchburg College

    Proponents of liberal education often claim that liberal learning serves as excellent preparation for citizenship and leadership.[1] The Association of American Colleges and Universities, for example, in its "Statement on Liberal Learning" asserts: "A truly liberal education is one that that prepares us to live responsible, productive, and creative lives in a dramatically changing world." By enabling people to think more clearly, to express themselves "rigorously and creatively," to accept social responsibility, and to yearn for the truth, liberal learning constitutes "society's best investment in our shared future." Perusing promotional material sent out by liberal arts colleges to prospective students or reading their mission statements, one encounters variations on these themes. Thus my own institution is not unique in asserting a mission to prepare students for "intelligent and wholehearted participation in a global society and for effective leadership . . ." in part through a grounding in the liberal arts and sciences (*Lynchburg College Catalogue*, 2003-2004, 17).
    While these statements focus on the impact of liberal learning in a general way, others focus on the leadership lessons that come from reading certain "classic" texts, the very heart of liberal education. John

Clemens and Douglas Mayer, in their book, *The Classic Touch: Lessons in Leadership from Homer to Hemingway*, write: these "great books of history, biography, philosophy, and drama . . . constitute the collective wisdom of mankind" and "offer rich perspectives on the job of leading." From them one can glean "timeless and time-tested" lessons for leadership (xiii-xiv). Clemens and Mayer's applications focus on leadership in business enterprises, but they readily suggest the broader applicability of their analyses.

What I wish to suggest in this paper, however, is that a careful reading of Herman Melville's short novel *Billy Budd* should give us pause about these arguments. Connecting liberal learning and leadership is not unproblematic. In the novel, we find three characters placed along a moral and intellectual continuum. At one pole is Billy, "a sort of upright barbarian," an Adam before the Fall; at the other pole is John Claggert, the master-at-arms, "in whom was the mania of an evil nature." Somewhere between them is Captain the Honorable Edward Fairfax Vere, a "sailor of distinction," "an officer mindful of the welfare of his men," and a man "with a marked leaning toward everything intellectual." Vere is a paragon of liberal learning, a lover of books, whose library at sea consists of works "to which every serious mind of superior order occupying any active post of authority in the world naturally inclines." Yet Vere is also the one who knowingly condemns the innocent Billy to hang (52, 76, 60).

Morally speaking, Vere seems closer to Billy than to Claggert: they both care for the truth, have regard for others, and act courageously and temperately, each "radically sharing the rarer qualities of our nature" (115). Claggert, on the other hand, falsely accuses Billy of involvement in mutiny out of inordinate jealousy of Billy's goodness and beauty. "Apprehending the good, but powerless to be it," Claggert finds himself captive to the passions within him that must see Billy destroyed (78). Yet with respect to education, Billy is on one side, and Vere and Claggert are on the other. Billy is illiterate, a seaman with little sense of the corrupt ways of landsmen. Vere, for his part, never went to sea without a "newly replenished library." His taste ran to "books treating of actual men and events no matter of what era— history, biography, and unconventional writers like Montaigne, who, free from cant and convention, honestly and in the spirit of common sense philosophize upon realities" (62). Claggert's manner, like Vere's, suggests an education and career "incongruous with his naval function." Also aloof, secretive, and self-contained, Claggert is the only one besides the captain intellectually capable of appreciating the moral phenomenon presented in Billy Budd. Yet he uses his intellectual powers to serve insane ends. While his evil nature is not the result of "vicious training," "corrupting books," or "licentious living," neither does his education transform that nature (76).

With education comes cleverness of speech, even eloquence; Billy's "flaw" is a speech defect, an inability to express himself under pressure. Confronted by Claggert's false accusation, the foretopman can only lash out physically, striking his accuser in the forehead—the home of the intellect. By contrast, Captain Vere is the learned speaker—who turns his skills to the task of convincing the drumhead court that Billy must hang.

Melville's reveals the ambiguity about Vere in other ways. Skeptical of the master-at-arms' charge of mutiny, Vere calls Billy in and has Claggert repeat his accusation. Noticing Billy's speech difficulty, Vere lays "a soothing hand" on the sailor's shoulder and addresses him in a "fatherly" manner: "There is no hurry, my boy. Take your time, take your time" (99). Further, the Captain reassures Billy before the drumhead court that he believes Billy innocent of mutinous intent and, again, reacts as might be expected of a loving father.

Against these positive portrayals come more negative characterizations. The narrator cites in Vere "little appreciation of mere humor" and a reputation among his peers for "lacking in the companionable quality." Besides being too serious and perhaps too removed from the crew, Vere had "a queer streak of pedantry running through him" and settled convictions that were "as a dike against those invading waters of novel opinion" (62). More serious is Vere's rush to judgment: no sooner had the ship's surgeon verified that Claggert was indeed dead than Vere already had decided: "Struck dead by an angel of God! Yet the angel must hang!" (101). No wonder that the surgeon leaves the cabin, "full of disquietude and misgiving." What follows in the narrative is a brief exploration of the boundaries of sanity and insanity and an invitation to the reader to decide whether Captain Vere "as the surgeon professionally and privately surmised," had suffered a sudden case of temporary insanity. Finally, by invoking the law of the Mutiny Act, which cannot take into account the intentions of the accused, Vere calls attention to the limits of law. As an educated man himself drawn to books, Vere perhaps too easily finds appealing the literalness of the King's Law.

What then does liberal learning contribute to the practice of leadership? In this instance, at least, readers may sense the author's ambivalence about the value of liberal education. The "Melvillean" critique of the liberal education-leadership link that emerges from this discussion includes the following three points. First, liberal education tends to distance people from each other and leaders from those they lead. The "critical thinking" skills prized by liberal arts practitioners result in a setting-apart of one from the other and the attenuation of more natural fellow feeling that might otherwise exist among people. Billy's untutored good nature does more to bring about harmony on board the *Bellipotent* than anything Claggert or Vere does. For them, force and fraud are necessary elements in maintaining order on board ship. To be sure, part of the distance between the officers and the crew exists by virtue of the different roles each must play. Nevertheless, even Captain Vere's peers sense in him "a lack of companionable quality" and nickname him "Starry Vere," an appropriate appellation for one often found "standing alone on the weather-side of the quarter-deck" staring absently at the blank sea (61).

Secondly, an enhanced capacity for self-expression does not necessarily mean one has made moral progress; mastery of a body of knowledge is not a substitute for good character. With liberal learning comes greater self-consciousness; out of that heightened sense of self flow ambition and the desire for fame, passions the narrator suggests Vere may have secretly indulged (129).

Third, liberal education may make a leader too reliant on books or a set of rules to deal with problems that arise. Vere's intellectual bent may make him too susceptible to act in accordance with certain theoretical categories, perhaps inappropriately. The mind trained to search out general principles may be too quick to see patterns where none exist or to overlook important particulars that would otherwise mar theoretical elegance.

On the other hand, Vere's learning heightens his—and our—sense of the tragic in political life. Liberal learning may contribute to better leadership in some ways, but it should also recognize the limits of its contribution as well, leaving room for experience and for the realm of practice. As Clemens and Mayer say of what the classics can teach about leadership:

> Leading, it turns out, is much more than formulas and techniques, accounting and computers. Leaders work in a world where

contradiction is commonplace, where today's right answer is tomorrow's disaster—a world in which hunch, intuition, experience, openness to untested ideas, and certainly self-assurance are more important to success than mere technical skills. The art of leading is the art of being human." (xiv)

Notes

1. I use "liberal learning," "liberal education," and "liberal arts" interchangeably in this paper. I realize that each of these may encompass somewhat different subject matter, but do not believe that taking account of those differences would materially affect the paper's argument.

Works Cited

American Association of Colleges and Universities. "Statement on Liberal Learning." <<http://www.aacu.org/about/statements/-liberal_learning.cfm>>.

Clemens, John K. and Mayer, Douglas. *The Classic Touch: Lessons in Leadership from Homer to Hemingway.* Homewood, Illinois: Dow Jones-Irwin, 1987.

Karcher, Carolyn. *Shadow Over the Promised Land: Slavery, Race, and Violence in Melville's America.* Baton Rouge: Louisiana State UP, 1980.

Lynchburg College. "Mission Statement." Lynchburg College Catalogue, 2004-2004.

Melville, Herman. *Billy Budd: Sailor (An Inside Narrative).* Eds. Harrison Hayford and Merton Sealts. Chicago: U Chicago P, 1962.

Scorza, Thomas J. *In The Time Before Steamships: Billy Budd, the Limits of Politics, and Modernity.* DeKalb, Ill.: Northern Illinois UP, 1979.

"Shall I Ever Attain My Heart's Desire?" or How a Flexible Approach to Core Texts is Building Layers of Community at Hanover College

Jeffrey Brautigam
Hanover College

"Shall I ever attain my heart's desire?" asks a human voice, breaking for just a moment the midnight quiet of the forest. When the voice repeats the question a second time, the following exchange takes place between the human voice and the "voice from above":
"What can you sacrifice to win your heart's desire?"
"My Life itself!"
"Life is so insignificant that it is the simplest thing for anyone to sacrifice!"
"What more have I? What else to offer?"
"Devotion! my friend, devotion!" declared the voice from above.[1]

That exchange takes place in the brief "Prologue" to Bankim Chandra Chatterji's novel *Anandamath* (about which I shall have more to say in a moment), but it might just as easily refer to a conversation between our Dean and whatever "voice from above" watches over the Hanover College community. For our Dean has indeed displayed a sense of unwavering devotion in her campaign to prod and cajole the faculty into implementing the new curriculum called for by the new Academic Vision Plan for Hanover College. Ratified by the faculty and approved by the Board of Trustees in the fall of 2002, the plan calls for, among other things, a comprehensive overhaul of general degree requirements for all students. The new requirements, known as Liberal Arts Degree Requirements (LADRs), require each student to take 14 integrated, collaborative courses which are organized around thematic categories that are directly related to the fundamental questions and objectives of the liberal arts and that are shared among different disciplines. The end result will be a kind of core curriculum that is far more collaborative and interdisciplinary than before.

One of the desired results of the new, interdisciplinary curriculum is a more cohesive and more broadly intellectual sense of community for our campus. Preliminary results from this curricular experiment may, therefore, offer a tentative answer to the series of questions about the relationship between core-text courses and the creation of culture and communities that are at the heart of this year's conference theme. The answers that I am going to offer here come from my experience this past year teaching in the Great Works LADR.

Rather than create one Great Works course around a single reading list (thereby ensnaring ourselves in a web of inclusion/exclusion issues), Hanover College has chosen to allow participating faculty to create their own versions of two-semester, team-taught, interdisciplinary Great Works courses, selecting texts and themes that correspond to their own expertise and interests. What these courses have in common is a set of objectives aimed at engendering inquiry into the issues that form the core of Great Works debates. Specifically, all Great Works courses must push the group (twelve students and two faculty members) to propose and examine criteria for discussing what makes a work "great," and to articulate whether there are enduring, objective standards for the evaluation of human products and inventions, or whether all such criteria are culturally constructed and historically contingent.

This past year, in collaboration with Kay Stokes of the English Department, I taught a Great Works course titled "Creativity in Conflict: Great Works in the British Empire." Central to the course and, I would argue, to Imperialism and Post-Colonialism are issues of identity and community. A text that has proven most useful in producing thoughtful discussion about those issues is Chatterji's *Anandamath*. Chaterji (1838-1894) is often referred to as the "founder of the Bengali novel" and as a "crucial force" in the creation of Hindu nationalism.[2] The novel, originally written in Bengali in 1882, captured the imagination of a new generation of Indian nationalists when Basanta Kumar Roy produced a new English translation in 1941. *Anadamath* is set in late 18th-century India against a backdrop of famine. In a plot loosely based on the *sanyasi* revolt, a band of ascetic warriors known as "the Children" wage a guerilla war to liberate "Mother India" from the puppet potentates and Sepoy soldiers of the British East India Company. These exploits are accompanied by much singing of the "Bande Mataram"—a nationalist hymn of Chatterji's own composition, which would become an anthem of the nationalist movement.[3]

As the tale unfolds, several characters representing different strata and niches of Indian society are drawn into the rebellion and forced to contemplate the meaning of identity and community. For example, Mahendra Singh, a wealthy *zamindar* (land owner/landlord), must decide whether or not to give up his duties to his family in order to join "the Children" and serve Mother India for the duration of the struggle. Then there is the case of Shanti, the daughter of a Brahmin professor of Sanskrit, who, having grown up motherless, never learned to dress or act like a girl. When, later in life, her husband Jiban disappears to join "the Children," Shanti adopts a male disguise and follows him. When her true identity is discovered, the warriors must decide what elements are crucial to the identity of "the Children." That is, they must decide if Shanti is disqualified by her gender as tradition would dictate, or whether her proven abilities and dedication to the cause have earned her membership.

The message of *Anandamath*—that a combination of great sacrifice and great unity is necessary to create a great community— seems to generate both excitement and anxiety in everyone who reads it. The Academic Vision Plan, with its similar message, has had something of the same effect on the faculty. Faculty not trained in the study of literature, for example, worry whether they have the expertise to evaluate and teach "Great Works." They worry too that so much interdisciplinary teaching will hurt the cohesiveness of their traditional community—their academic department. They worry, in short, about issues of identity and community. But the past year's experience tells me that they should not worry so much. The effects produced by team-teaching an interdisciplinary course and by engaging in genuine inquiry with a colleague and twelve students for two full semesters are of the identity enriching and community building variety. And, the past year's experience also tells me that those effects are being felt on every level of human interaction at Hanover College.

For example, research tells us that one of the primary causes of first-year-class attrition is the failure of the student to find a sense of community within the College. The twelve first-year students that I spent the past year with have, I believe, managed to find that community; and they have found it, at least in part, in their Great Works class. Or, more accurately, those twelve students who have spent the entire year working on a single set of issues, sharing readings and discussions with each other and with the same two professors, have forged a community of their own. Additionally, those students, by virtue of spending an entire year with Professor Stokes and myself and by coming to understand that they are genuinely participating in active inquiry with us, have relationships with us that are richer than normal for first-year students. They are frequent visitors to our offices; they greet us in the dining areas and around campus; they have met and played with our child; and they have had, in some cases, their first taste of Indian food in our home.

Participation in the Great Works and other LADR courses has also strengthened, rather than weakened, a sense of community within departments. In my department (the Department of History), this communal solidarity initially took the form of "circling the wagons" to defend our major curriculum from the Dean's encroaching hand. But eventually, after reminding ourselves that we, as faculty members, were the authors of the Vision Plan and the architects of the LADR curriculum, we began to see our new, interdisciplinary teaching as both an opportunity and a model for redesigning and reinvigorating our major. Additionally, the faculty members teaching within the Great Works LADR are slowly forming a community of their own. Concerns about expertise and identity are fading as conversations about texts, techniques, and results become easier and more frequent.

about expertise and identity are fading as conversations about texts, techniques, and results become easier and more frequent.

Finally, even that great communal and cultural chasm that divides the faculty identity from the administrative identity is being bridged. Individual faculty from departments across the College are working easily with faculty designated as LADR coordinators. The coordinators are working seamlessly with newly constituted division heads. And, all are following the lead of our Dean, feeling, perhaps for the first time, that we are at last all pulling together and working tirelessly for a noble vision. Or, perhaps that is just a dream; and like the protagonists in Chatterji's *Anandamath*, our new community is still too young and fragile to achieve it. But the dream survives. "Devotion! my friend, devotion!"

Notes

1. Quotations from Bankim Chandra Chatterji, *Anandamath*.
2. See, for example, Tanika Sarkar, "Imagining Hindurashstra: the Hindu and the Muslim in Bankim Chandra's Writings."
3. The novel contains the lyrics for a song, the "Bande (or Vande) Mataram" (Hail Motherland), that Chatterji originally wrote in 1876. It became the slogan of the Indian National Congress and an anthem of the nationalist movement. However, because the national identity that *Anandamath* attempts to create is an unabashedly Hindu one, the song was not adopted as the Indian National Anthem. See "Chatterjee, Bankim Chandra," *The Columbia Encyclopedia*.

Works Cited

Chatterji, Bankim Chandra. *Anandamath*. New Delhi: Orient Paperbacks, 1992.

"Chatterjee, Bankim Chandra." *The Columbia Encyclopedia*, 6th Ed. New York: Columbia UP, 2004. <http://www.encyclopedia.com/>.

Sarkar, Tanika. "Imagining Hindurashstra: the Hindu and the Muslim in Bankim Chandra's Writings." *Making India Hindu*. Ed. David Ludden. Oxford: Oxford UP, 2005.

Educating for Justice: Service Learning and Plato's *Republic*

Jane Kelley Rodeheffer
Saint Mary's University of Minnesota

In guiding undergraduates through Plato's *Republic*, the approach taken by many professors is that of viewing the dialogue through the lens of its most famous image: the dramatic freeing of the prisoner from the world of shadows and appearances to which he has been chained and forcibly dragging him into the sun until his eyes become accustomed to true light of the Good itself. Socrates identifies both himself and his interlocutors as prisoners: "They're like us," he tells Glaucon and Adeimantus (515a). In identifying himself and his interlocutors with the prisoners of the cave, Socrates is suggesting that in order for just leadership to arise within a democracy, even philosophically predisposed citizens "like us" must be freed from the accepted opinion and bias to which we are easily enslaved. In a fast-moving democratic regime, which Socrates compares to "a many-colored cloak decorated in all hues" in which "all [pleasures] are alike and must be honored on an equal basis," sustained inquiry into the just life for citizens is difficult if not impossible (557c, 561c). In what follows, I will argue that the inquiry called the *Republic* remains an essential text for the education of just citizens, particularly when it is read within the context of an intentional community dedicated to such dialogue.

In a university setting, immersion in such a dialogical community can be achieved by placing two very different experiences in tension: a close reading of the *Republic* itself with service learning in the local community, in which questions of justice are allowed to arise in the context of, for example, tutoring truant adolescents in an alternative school, incarcerated adolescents in the facility Bob Dylan made famous in his "Walls of Red Wing," or visiting elderly Alzheimer patients in an extended care facility. The combination of an intentional community dedicated to dialogue about great texts and service learning can create a context in which students can go beyond the notion of justice as a purely legal or political question and begin to attend to the becoming of justice in their own souls, which often takes the form of insights into the nature of the just life, the Good, and their own roles as citizens.

The *Republic* develops a dynamic tension between the city that is created in speech—the ideal city—and the city that is coming to be in the souls of Glaucon and Adeimantus as a result of their dialogue about the ideal city. Seth Benardette refers to this second city as the "dialogic city," since it arises from the action of dialogue upon the soul, including the soul of the reader. By tracing the deepening self-knowledge of Glaucon, we can see how the dialogue about the just city allows the philosophical *eros* inherent in Glaucon's soul to break free of its bondage to his tyrannical *eros*—his longing for power and control—and the implications of that breaking free for students engaged in service learning in the community.

In order to show Socrates that the unjust life is superior to the just one, Glaucon tells a story that provides us with a window into his soul (358e-362c). It is the story of the shepherd Gyges, who discovers a ring that makes him invisible, thus allowing him to see what usually remains hidden, and ultimately to seize power and rule the kingdom. Like his hero Gyges, Glaucon wants nothing to be hidden from himself; nothing should remain private or unknowable. As Socrates and Glaucon go on to discuss the requirements of the just regime, Glaucon rejects the Spartan design of the first city, calling it a "city of pigs" (372d). He wants luxuries, and he wants the guardians of the city to go to war because war is a means to power and the fulfillment of tyrannical appetites.

Glaucon's *eros* is not entirely tyrannical, however, for his desire to provoke Socrates into giving a defense of justice suggests that he is also possessed of a philosophical *eros*. It is this aspect of his character that allows for the moderating of his tyrannical desires and ultimately for a more just ordering of his soul. Glaucon knows that there is a disjunction between the appearance of justice, which seems weak and ineffectual when compared with injustice, and the true form of justice, and he says that he wants to see "what power it has all alone by itself when it is in the soul—dismissing its wages and its consequences" (358b). This desire to see justice abstracted from the existential complexities of human life allows students to recognize, as early as book II of the *Republic*, that the becoming of justice in Glaucon's soul will involve a struggle between his tyrannical *eros* and the philosophical *eros* that seeks the pure form of the Good.

Socrates sees this potential in Glaucon, for he suggests in book II that both Glaucon and Adeimantus are not persuaded by the arguments that they give in favor of the unjust life. Even while they are able to project the image of the unjust man, as in the figure of Gyges, Socrates knows that, "something divine must have happened to you if you are remaining unpersuaded that injustice is better than justice when you are able to speak that way on its behalf" (368a). In the words of Plato's *Seventh Letter*, Glaucon's true inner conviction—his justice—is "a divine spark which makes philosophy congenial to him and fits him for its pursuit" (340). It is equally clear, however, that Glaucon's inner conviction that the just life is the best life, needs a *logos*. Socrates knows this, but Glaucon must recognize his need of philosophic education, and this will not occur unless he descends by dialogue into the depths of the human soul. The creation of the ideal city is meant to show Glaucon that the life of the tyrant is not only seductive but also dangerous because it is unexamined, and thus closed in upon itself. For human community to flourish, the *eros* of Glaucon, like that of Plato's readers, must be opened and turned toward the quest for shared logos of the just life.

In the process of reading and discussing the *Republic* in an intentional community, some students discover, like Glaucon, a mysterious longing in their own souls for completion, a desire to give a *logos* to that "something quite divine" in themselves that the reading of this text, together with service learning, has begun to awaken. This longing is evidenced in the reflection of a student who spent the year visiting three elderly women on the Alzheimer's floor of a local extended care facility. After visiting a resident named Ruth for a number of weeks, the student began to wonder if Ruth really remembered her from week to week, as she seemed to indicate, or rather, if "she had just become good at reading people as she got used to her disease." In a later reflection, the student related that "there is another part of me, however, that knows she remembers me." The student wrote,

> In thinking about Ruth and the other residents I visit, I sometimes questioned what the point of my spending time with them was. I knew that they would forget me within the next hour. But spending time with Ruth these last few weeks made me wonder if the human soul, independent of the mind, somehow has knowledge of this love and interaction. Although I know she cannot truly remember me in her mind, perhaps she has some other knowledge, stored within her soul that does remember me, the kind of knowledge Socrates thinks that Glaucon and Adeimantus have. Somewhere, deep down inside of her, I have fulfilled a void of love and interaction. Although perhaps not in this world, this time, or this life, somewhere inside of Ruth, she knows me and holds me close to her heart.

Like Glaucon, whose moments of awareness in the *Republic* signal the beginning of his soul's ascent to wisdom, this student has begun to articulate her service activity according to a broader, more philosophic desire. Naïve idealism about "visiting the elderly" has given way to an articulation of the other's soul, and its relation to her own, in all of their complexity. In the context of reading the *Republic*, she had begun to realize that perhaps she was drawn to this activity for another more mysterious, but ultimately more genuine, "Good."

The end of the *Republic* provides another point of encounter for students engaged in service learning, an encounter that has particular implications for students tutoring incarcerated adolescents. In book X, Socrates tells a story attributed to a man named Er, who came back to life as he lay on his funeral pyre and recounted what he had seen of the various lots awaiting the soul in the next world. Socrates' explanation of this story is directed to the awakening of philosophical *eros* in both Glaucon and in the reader. He argues that the most important choice for a human soul in both life and death is to avoid tyranny, evil, and suffering by becoming a student of those who will give the soul "the capacity to know and to distinguish the good and the best life, and so everywhere and always to choose the better from among those that are possible" (618c). Socrates calls the capacity for making such distinctions *phronesis* (prudence), and he says that it requires taking into account "how in combination and separately" things like poverty and wealth, sickness and health, habits, facility in learning, "and all such things that are connected with a soul by nature or are acquired" may "affect the virtue of a life" (618c-d). When students who tutor incarcerated adolescents encounter this section of the text in seminar, they are often able to relate it to the unfolding story of the young men they are working with. In his final reflection on service learning in light of The *Republic*, one student wrote,

> When I began tutoring Jason in Math, I didn't understand why he was in prison. I thought a delinquent kid would act differently, but he seemed really motivated to learn and improve himself. The more Jason told me about his background on the reservation in Northern Minnesota, however, the more I understood why he ended up at Red Wing, which is pretty much the end of the line for adolescent offenders in this state. I don't know if I made any difference in Jason's life, but he certainly made a difference in mine. I think we connected, and he no longer fits my earlier stereotype of either a "juvenile delinquent" or a "deprived reservation kid." He's just a guy who's been through a lot and made some pretty awful choices, like those souls at the end of the *Republic*. Socrates says that those without education in philosophy, such souls would probably choose as their next life "the greatest tyranny, and, due to folly and gluttony, [choose] without having considered everything adequately" (619 b). I don't know if incarceration counts as education in philosophy, but it certainly has made Jason capable of making better choices. His performance in the tutoring program was so good that he qualified for Driver's education, and he hopes that if he gets his license and his GED, he will have a shot at getting a job when he gets out. While our plans and goals are different, I hope he reaches his and that I was a positive presence for him. We all need that hope.

According to Socrates retelling of the myth of Er, the capacity to know and distinguish the best life requires that the activity or labor of philosophy be pursued not in abstraction, but in the context of a community in which the labor of others can be witnessed. And not only their labor, but also their suffering, for the Greek word *peponêkotas* (from *ponêo*) means both labor and suffering (619d). To the extent that this student understood both Jason's suffering and the degree to which it affected "the virtue of [his] life," he was himself educated in practical wisdom, an education that was reinforced by his engagement with the *Republic*.

In the story that Er recounts, those few souls who had spent their lives firmly planted on the earth, were able to avoid the evil of choosing too quickly a tyrannical life, "because they themselves had labored and had seen the labor of others, [and] weren't in a rush to make their choices" (619d). This latter statement is very important for understanding both the *Republic's* account of justice and the saliency of involving students in service learning. It is here that the text points outside itself to lived experience, of the kind service learning allows. Socrates last words underscore the importance of both *praxis* and a community of dialogue for living the best life. He tells Glaucon that the happiest life is the one in which we "practice justice with prudence in every way, so that we shall be friends to ourselves and the gods" (621c).

I have tried to suggest that education for just citizenship begins in a close reading of the *Republic,* in an intentional community in which prudence is also being developed by students laboring and seeing the labor of others—whether they be truant and incarcerated adolescents or elderly patients in the Alzheimer's unit of a local nursing home. For it is only in such a truly dialogical community that the "tale of justice" Socrates speaks of at the end of the Republic could be "saved and not lost," and could even "save us, if we were persuaded by it" (621c).

Works Cited

Benardette, Seth. *Socrates' Second Sailing: On Plato's* Republic. Chicago: U of Chicago P, 1989.

Plato. *Plato's Seventh Letter.* Trans. Walter Hamilton. New York: Penguin Books, 1973.

Plato. *The Republic of Plato.* Trans. Allen Bloom. New York: Basic Books, 1991.

Bridging the Gaps Between
the Humanities and Sciences

Natural Philosophy as a Liberal Art

J.H. Beall
St. John's College, Annapolis

Introductory Comments

Our studies have brought us together to investigate some common threads in old books. Many in the modern world do not subscribe to our methods, however. To them, these old books are like ghosts. They seem insubstantial when compared face to face with the dread miracle of the present moment. For example, what possible relevance could studying Thucydides' *Peloponnesian War* have for America in the 21st Century?

To some, it seems that reading old books is like wandering through a landscape of shadows. They don't know the secret, but you remember it, revealed in the scene from Homer's *Odyssey*. The hero has gone far into a cold north in order to find a way home. He must *give to the dead the blood of the living* (Homer 90-110) in order that those shades can speak true and tell him of the hazards he must face to return safely to his homeland.

In a very real sense, the way in which we study core texts is in fact giving a nod to Homer's metaphor about the blood of the living. By the way, I am grateful to Eva Brann for first promulgating Homer's dictum in a lecture at St. John's a few years ago. Such studies take time, energy, and commitment; bespeak of esoteric interests; and admit of a certain remove from the exigencies of the work-a-day world. Yet they are labors of high seriousness, nonetheless.

It is not too much to say that simple words, geometric constructions, and mathematical formulas (sometimes very old words, antiquarian constructions, and more recent formulas) have changed the world. To understand the trajectories of history, the evolution of thought, indeed to understand words and ideas themselves, requires some regard for the history of ideas. And the best way to do this is to read original texts.

The enterprise of reading core texts has always struck me as a recapitulation, a kind of pilgrimage through an evolution of different stations of thought. Those who study Euclid have the tools necessary to study Ptolemy. And Ptolemy is remarkable in the context of this discussion because his is literally the first mathematical theory of the movements of the world. He was clearly an inspiration to Copernicus and Kepler, to Leibniz, Newton, and Taylor, and by their heritage, to all of mathematical physics.

If we can consider contemporary thought (and I include mathematical physics in this category) as the result of an evolution of ideas that we have inherited from our ancestors (intellectual or otherwise), then it seems incumbent upon us to make a considered attempt to go through the argument and to provide our students with a similar opportunity. Otherwise, we are likely not to know what we are saying when we speak, nor will we completely comprehend our own thoughts. To quote Darwin (and perhaps not so much out of context as it might seem):

> When we no longer look at an organic being as a savage looks at a ship, as at something wholly beyond his comprehension, when we regard every production of nature as one which has had a history; when we contemplate every complex structure and instinct as a summing up of many contrivances, each useful to the possessor, nearly in the same way as when we look at any great mechanical invention as the summing up of the labour, the experience, the reason, and even the blunders of numerous workmen; when we thus view each organic being; how far more interesting...will the study of natural history become! (Chap. XIV, 456)

If we are able to see the origins of our ideas, then we can have a deeper understanding of them. By implication, if we fail to understand the inherited structures of our thoughts and ideas, we risk being like Darwin's old "savage," unable to distinguish form from function, mere appearance from truth.

The necessity to go through an argument, to recapitulate it, to make it live by giving it our living blood, extends to the whole of the ideas that constitute the modern world. And this clearly includes the central core of ideas that represent (to my mind) one of the greatest intellectual constructions of humankind, that body of work we currently term mathematical physics. For its intrinsic beauty, its stern and forbidding symbolic landscape, and its curious utility, it has few equals.

It is perhaps less obvious that it has implications for us, for the way we think about ourselves as creatures and creators. But my belief is that it is in fact possible to entertain such a thesis. In part, this is why I have chosen the peculiar title of this talk to be "Natural Philosophy as a Liberal Art." Before trying to bring some light to this, it is clearly incumbent upon me to define my terms.

Definitions

A "liberal art" in the old sense of the phrase is one of those that helps to liberate the human soul from its passions, those things suffered from without or from within, but beyond the realm of a reasoned pattern of life. A liberal art is one that makes a human soul free: from those elemental conditions in which it finds itself and that traffic with its fears, from limitations that prevent it from being self-determining. A free man or woman is one who is capable of living a reasoned and productive life, a life not driven by passions that would circumscribe horizons and delimit the individual toward the mere animal. Again, since this is esoteric, we can find no modern examples of people who are consumed by their own passions, but history does provide us with quite a few cases to study.

There has been a great deal said about the liberal (or liberating) arts. Since I am from St. John's College, I cannot resist mentioning the College Seal, which symbolizes one characterization of them. I note that they involve grammar, rhetoric, and logic (the trivium), and arithmetic, geometry, music, and astronomy (the quadrivium).

It is perhaps more difficult to define natural philosophy. But parsing the terms a bit, philosophy is the love of wisdom. Not the holding of it, mind you (for love in many ways is a realization of the necessity of both the taking up and the letting go), but the *love* of wisdom. The term "natural" likely has to do with the nature of things. So natural philosophy could be considered as the love of a wisdom about the nature of things or, more colloquially, of natural things.

Newton is in many ways the author who has given natural philosophy its present character as mathematical physics. Newton's wonderful clockwork in the *Mathematical Principles of Natural Philosophy*[1] (or the *Principia* as it is known) shows natural philosophy as that author conceives it. Leibniz and Taylor belong firmly in this Pantheon, also, and I will try to make brief mention of them a bit later, but in the interests of brevity, I will use Newton as my primary focus.

It would seem to be fair at first gloss (especially given our preceding discussion) to think of Newton's mechanics (i.e., Natural Philosophy) as a liberal art. There are present in the *Principia* wide and magnificent landscapes of geometry and arithmetic in his view of uniform and accelerated motions. The entire Calculus that he invents (Volume II of the *Principia*) for the occasion of his study of the "System of the World" (presented in Volume III), is entirely about "number in time," and the "System of the World" is revelatory about the nature of the orbits of the planets around the sun and of Jupiter's and Saturn's moons about their respective centers. As a system of logical deduction, the *Principia* is quite beautiful. And of course, the rhetorical force of Newton's argument and its grammatical excellence are parts of our history and worthy of emulation.

I will give some few examples of Newton's consideration of orbits to show his method, and in the process, I believe that you will see that arithmetic, geometry, astronomy, and even music are fundamental to the *Principia*. It also has undeniable elements of logic, grammar, and rhetoric in it. In sum, the *Principia* has all of the elements that we normally associate with the liberal arts.

While we will not have time for a discussion of it here, I recommend a perusal of Newton's "Scholium on Absolute Space and Time" in the *Principia*. In that portion of the *Principia*, Newton raises Natural Philosophy to a level that informs Metaphysics, and it is not accidental that much of Newton's disagreement with Leibniz rests on Newton's disinclination to give up the idea of absolute space and time.

Newton's treatment of the motion of bodies (the laws of motion)

After the Scholium on Absolute Space and Time, Newton gives us his certifiably famous laws of motion. I will remind you of them only briefly and to the extent necessary to show how they and the first Corollary following them are used to discuss orbits. I will use these to demonstrate the mathematical nature of the *Principia*. With the help of some of Brooke Taylor's work, we could show how this can lead to a mathematical analysis of music. Unfortunately, we will not have time for it in this paper. The laws of motion are as follows:

> 1. Every body continues in its state of rest, or of uniform motion in a right line, unless it is compelled to change that state by forces impressed upon it." (2)

Newton's commentary follows in the *Principia*, but does not concern us too much here. I only want to remark that the law suggests something important about motion, that it is preserved unless opposed. This property leads Leibniz to an investigation of the principles related to what we now call momentum and kinetic energy. The real point is that the persistence of motion is not something one observes in terrestrial phenomena. The fact that Newton makes no distinction between terrestrial and astronomical phenomena is remarkable. The Second Law is the basis for a considerable amount of modern mechanics.

> 2. The change of motion is proportional to the motive force impressed; and is made in the direction of the right line in which that force is impressed.

This is the source of the famous $F = ma$, that is, force equals mass times acceleration.

The Third Law has applications in statics as well as mechanics, and states that

> 3. To every action there is always opposed an equal reaction; or the mutual actions of two bodies upon each other are always equal, and directed to contrary parts.

This is one of the audience participation parts: Press your fingers together—thumb to index finger is fine. Do you feel the contrary part pressing back? Of course. The joke among physics graduate students is that this makes you feel "wanted."

Newton has several corollaries and a scholium after the three Laws of Motion, but only Corollary I will occupy us here. However, it is quite important. It can be illustrated by the parallelogram shown in Figure 1, and Newton's commentary on the diagram is quite lucid. Corollary I states that

> A body, acted on by two forces simultaneously, will describe the diagonal of a parallelogram in the same time as it would describe the sides by those forces separately. (1)

Two forces act on a body at the point A. One force can produce a velocity that will carry the body along AB in a given time, while the other force can produce a velocity that will carry the body along AC in the same time. The forces acting together will produce a velocity that carries the body along the diagonal, AD. The resolution of forces is geometric, and this is such a commonplace to us that it is not as surprising as it ought to be. Every physics student knows Corollary I as the "force table" diagram.

Newton's treatment of the motion of bodies (orbits and centripetal forces)

Newton then uses the laws of motion in conjunction with Corollary I to establish a set of theorems about centripetal forces (i.e., center-seeking forces, or forces directed toward a center) and how different kinds of forces yield different relationships between the size of the orbit and the time it takes for the body to complete the path around the center of force.

Figure 2 is associated with Proposition I, in Section II of the *Principia*. The proposition states that:

> The areas which revolving bodies describe by radii drawn to an immovable centre of force do lie in the same immovable planes, and are proportional to the times in which they are described.

The proof is beyond the scope of this talk, but I wanted to talk about it just a bit. If you look at the parallelogram BcCV in our Figure 2, you will see that it matches exactly the diagram for Corollary I. In fact, Newton's proof simply says that a body moving with a certain velocity will move through the distance AB in some particular time. If no force is applied to it, it will continue to move along the line Bc. The force of gravity, which he calls the centripetal force, acts along BV and produces a motion of the body from B to V in the same amount of time that the body takes to go from B to c. The net result, by Corollary I, is a motion from B to C in that same time.

Newton uses this diagram, drawn along the path ABCDEF, to give a rough approximation of an orbit. If the units of time are taken to be smaller and smaller, the broken line becomes more and more like a curve. The central thesis of the calculus is that in the "limit," these sections actually become an arc, that is, a smooth curve or orbit from A to F. In this simple proposition (with the line segments increased in number and made smaller and smaller), Newton has already proved Kepler's Second Law.

Corollary I (the parallelogram of forces or velocities) is used as an *element* in Proposition I of Section II (the segmented curve diagram).

And for that matter, Newton's curved orbit for a planet drawn by the force of gravity from the Sun becomes elemental in Taylor's derivation of the wave equation, which describes the motion of a stretched string. Each of these examples shows that the separate deductions of the propositions are part of a *system* of logical thought.

I hope that by these few examples I have made a reasonable argument that the mathematical derivations in the *Principia* are part of a logical system. It should not be too much of a stretch for us to recognize the kindredness between these derivations and the rest of the *Principia*. We would find with sufficient time for study a "single, golden braid" of thought. But this clearly does not stop with Newton and the *Principia*, even including his "System of the World."

I intend to return to this theme in a moment, but first I can't resist saying a bit about how the *Principia* came about. It bears directly upon the nature of scientific investigation, both in its whimsy and its seriousness.

An anecdote about the how the *Principia* came to be

It is not long after Proposition I in Section II (a few pages, in actuality) that Newton proves the relation between the force law for gravity and Kepler's laws. Newton does this in Proposition IV of the same section. The problem of what Kepler's Laws tell us about how the Sun draws the planets was perhaps originally posed to Newton by Edmund Halley and Sir Christopher Wren. Wren offered a prize of a forty-shilling book for someone who could show what Kepler's Third Law implies for the way the force of gravity decreases with the distance from the attracting body (i.e., the Sun).

Kepler's Laws of themselves represent a triumph in the way in which observations of phenomena can be informed by mathematical thought. From the flux of experience, Kepler took Tycho Brahe's data on planetary orbits (itself a work of more than 20 years), and after another 20 years of analysis, deduced three laws that stated that the irregular appearance of planetary motion can be summarized with three simple rules:

1. The planets move in elliptical orbits with the sun at one focus.
2. A line from the sun to any planets sweeps out equal areas in equal time.
3. The square of a planet's period is proportional to the cube of the planet's mean distance from the sun (or more accurately, the planet's semi-major axis).

There are a number of web sites that provide animations of

Kepler's laws. David Austin's Java Applet illustrates and animates the three laws.[3] A perusal of Phenomenon IV in the *Principia*'s "System of the World" will demonstrate the consistency of the derived relationship between the orbital periods and radii with that obtained from observations.

It was this third law that was the focus of Wren's and Halley's interest. Newton is reputed to have responded to Halley's request by letter (he couldn't find the proof when Halley visited him). In a short letter, he outlined the proof that Kepler's Third Law implied that the force of gravity diminished as the inverse square of the distance (i.e. r^{-2}). Twice the distance away from the Sun implies 1/4 of the centripetal force.

In the *Principia* Newton does not stop at what nature actually *does*. By the time Newton has reached proposition IV of Section II (the determination of centripetal forces), he has demonstrated not only that he has solved Halley's problem of the force law for gravity implied by Kepler's Third Law, but he notes that he can determine the relation of period to radius of the orbit (i.e., the semi-major axis in the case of the ellipse) for *any* force law! The inverse-square force law becomes a special case of the much more general relations. Presumably, Newton has done his calculation to show that, if God had decided on a different law for universal gravitation, Newton was up to calculating that, too.

These parts of the *Principia* show the remarkable beauty of the mathematical relations of planetary orbits. Such a statement is genuinely stunning from a certain point of view, since it suggests that ponderable (and ponderous) bodies actually seem to follow such patterns. It is no wonder that after all the efforts to understand the natural world, the success of Natural Philosophy in the realm of planetary and satellite orbits produced a flowering of interest in such methods.

Natural Philosophy as a Logical System

In the foregoing remarks, I have tried to show some of the method of Natural Philosophy as Newton practices it. I have given some examples of how problems are first brought to the mind of an investigator. In many cases, the instigation for important research is simple wonder at how something could be so. But the 40-shilling book prize has many analogs, too. I hope that the scope of the investigation is apparent. I have provided the merest outline. Bacon's "Great Instauration" in *Novum Organum* is before us. We are not dealing here with a carefully confined and limited problem.

In the case of the *Principia*, Newton has the intellectual heritage of the *Almagest* and Plato's *Republic*. If one of these seems surprising, then I ask you to reflect on the 40 years of work it took to transform the shadows and traces on the sky (a particular kind of Cave, indeed!) into Kepler's laws and regularities. Those in turn led the natural philosopher to see the underlying causes. For Kepler's Second Law (equal areas in equal times), it was centripetal force. For Kepler's Third Law, it was the inverse-square law of universal gravitation.

So I do not limit this discussion to Ptolemy, Copernicus, Kepler, Newton, Leibniz, and Tayor. In some sense, the system of thought I call Natural Philosophy is still evolving, still adding elements to its complex and exciting structure.

To reminisce about the history of mathematical physics is rather much like looking at the trajectory of a body in its orbit. Each station of the orbit seems inevitable and occasions the next, just as each station of thought brings us to the next.

If Natural Philosophy can be thought of as a logical system, perhaps the strangest aspect of it is its curious relation to nature. While Socrates put the forms outside of the Cave (and perhaps ironically in the intelligible realm), Kant placed them within us. The laws of nature, like Kepler's Laws, do not admit of equivocation. Or do they? Well, the thing is not altogether desperate. We do have some hope that our logical systems of thought are unitary.

Let me say a bit more about this shortly. But first I want to remind us of a significant difficulty. These historic "stations of thought," which have proved so useful in the modern world, imply inevitability. The nascent ability to predict orbits and trajectories developed by Newton led Laplace to state that:

> We may regard the present state of the universe as the effect of its past and the cause of its future. An intellect which at any given moment knew all of the forces that animate nature and the mutual positions of the beings that compose it, if this intellect were vast enough to submit the data to analysis, could condense into a single formula the movement of the greatest bodies of the universe and that of the lightest atom; for such an intellect nothing could be uncertain and the future just like the past would be present before its eyes. (Laplace 2)

Thus, determinism enters into the realm of Natural Philosophy. What possible liberating influence can natural philosophy so defined have upon free people, and what can it mean that I associate Natural Philosophy with the Liberal Arts, those that aid in the liberation of the human soul?

The Lucretian swerve: breaking the bonds of necessity

The question is a serious one. Newton's mechanics in the *Principia* allow us to claim that if we know the position, velocity, and acceleration of a particle, then we will be able to predict its motion indefinitely into the future. The only uncertainty in the prediction of the trajectory of the particle is in the uncertainty of the measurements of these initial positions, speeds, and accelerations. If we know these (as we can in principle from a classical point of view), and we know the same information for all other particles, then the entire system of particles is utterly predictable in its behavior. There will be no surprises in the evolution of the system, and even if there were errors in calculations, the principle remains the same. The world is deterministic.

Having this as a consequence of a Natural Philosophy that is based on the Liberal Arts leads to rather uncomfortable conclusions, since it seems to do away with free will altogether. In this scheme, the only claim we have to the appearance of free will is that of ignorance. The only reason I cannot predict the behavior of the system is because I do not know all the things that affect it. Of course, this worry is not new.

The initial realization that a deterministic natural philosophy would be a problem for the concept of freedom is clearly mentioned a long way back in Lucretius's *On the Nature of Things*. In setting up his atomistic cosmology, consisting utterly of mechanism, Lucretius insists upon a "swerve" in the deterministic trajectories of atoms falling through an infinite void. He realizes that if everything is predictable, then in order to "break the bonds of necessity," there must be some random (or whimsical) element that makes it possible for the atoms (that we are made of) to not follow entirely deterministic paths. Otherwise, to repeat myself, any hope of freedom or the free will is simply illusion or ignorance.

But before we either despair or begin to appeal to esoteric things like the wave-particle duality and the Heisenberg uncertainty relations, let us investigate the nature of logical systems for a bit. One of the hallmarks of logical deduction is its certitude. But upon some reflection, we have indications that things are a bit more subtle than would seem at first to be the case. I do not intend to give an explicit discussion here, but a few examples are in order.

The first is in the Platonic dialog, *Parmenides*. Parmenides is shown as an ancient and venerable philosopher with Socrates as a young man, somewhat stymied before Parmenides. Another young man, Aristotles, is present. Aristotles is chosen as a participant in the latter part of the discussion because he is young and "will not make difficulties and will be the most likely to say what he thinks" (50). This has to be an ironic comment on Plato's part, since Aristotles goes on to become "one of the Thirty," that is, one of the Thirty Tyrants who ruled Athens after it capitulated to Sparta.

What Parmenides demonstrates to Aristotles is (apparently) that you can prove anything using reason—at least with regard to the One: the One both is and is not, it is Many and One, it is Becoming and not Becoming. The last comment in the dialog apparently has Aristotles saying, "Most true." Thus, a budding tyrant is shown that there is nothing that is true, and that truth is arbitrary. Reflecting on this, it is no wonder that Socrates is so worried about Meno's fate in the *Meno*. Meno clearly needs some direction. He poses his "quarrelsome" question to Socrates. To paraphrase, "Why search for truth? If I know it, I don't need to seek it, and if I don't know it, I wouldn't recognize it if it came up and bit me." To answer this, Socrates has only an appeal to the Gods or the whole substance of the doctrine of recollection.

The problem Parmenides illustrates resurfaces in Kant's antinomies in the *Critique of Pure Reason,* and in John Bell's response to Einstein, Podolski, and Rosen's argument against the completeness of quantum mechanics as a physical theory. Bell demonstrates the apparent contradiction between causal theories of nature, ideas of localization, and the speed of light as a limit on the rate of the transfer of information. My point in alluding to these ideas is not to explicate them, but to notice that there seem to be similarities between certain aspects of logical structures and theories of nature.

Actually, none of this should surprise us. The nature of logical systems has its most profound explication in the famous Godel theorems. A rough paraphrase might be as follows: any logical system can either be complete (in that all of its possible propositions are articulated) or consistent—but not both. Godel articulated these in response to Russell and Whitehead's *Principia Mathematica,* an attempt at formalism then in vogue to turn mathematical expositions into deterministic and predictable trajectories of thought.

Concluding remarks

If the language I am using seems similar to that I used to describe Laplace's idea of determinism, I admit it. I also note the similarity between Godel's and Bell's enterprises. Both are articulations that seem to belie the determinate and formal explication of the mathematical foundations of thought and experience.

In closing, I should say something about the possible resolution of such profound questions, but I admit that I can only ask them, and haltingly at that. What I have noticed and presented here are certain similarities between the nature of logical structures and the nature of Natural Philosophy. These might be extended through our current attempts to understand quantum mechanics. These contradictory articulations, these antinomies, seem to present themselves in hauntingly similar ways in philosophy, mathematics, and nature.

Where does this leave us? I could simply say that by studying nature we are studying ourselves—a task sufficient in itself because we have no hope of knowledge of *noumenal* things. Such a study of nature gives us some hope of freedom within our own cognitions. I could then claim to have given credence to the title of this talk. But such a position is so bitterly skeptical that I cannot claim it.

What I take to be the correct stance comes from Godel. He states that in any logical system (with some specifications on the system's robustness), it is possible to state propositions that you know to be true and yet cannot prove. I must thank Curtis Wilson, a colleague of mine at St. John's, for this distillation of Godel's thought.

What do I know to be true? Well, truth is very difficult. I believe that the hard anvil of necessity has shaped this system of thought that we call Natural Philosophy. Such a necessity suggests an underlying order beyond the world of phenomena. Furthermore, I believe that these antinomies, these dualities, which we see in ourselves and in nature, represent a fundamental kindredness between noumena, phenomena, and mind.

Notes

1. I am taking this and other quotes from the *Principia*, specifically from the 1729 Andrew Mott translation from the Latin, as modified by Florian Cajori. A version of the first portion of the Mott translation can be found on the web at <http://members.tripod.com/~gravitee/>.
2. David Austin's web page can be found at: <http://www.sunsite.ubc.ca/LivingMathematics/V001N01/UBCExamples/Kepler/kepler.html> Another illustrative web site can be found at <http://www.phy.ntnu.edu.tw/java/Kepler/Kepler.html>

Works Cited

Darwin, Charles. *The Origin of Species by Means of Natural Selection.* Chapter XIV. New York: Penguin Classics, 1982.

Homer. *The Odyssey.* Trans. Robert Fagles. New York: Penguin, 1999.
Kant, Emmanuel. *Critique of Pure Reason.* Trans. Norman Kemp Smith. New York: St. Martin's Press, 1969.
Laplace. Preface. *Philosophical Essay on Probabilities: Sources in the History of Mathematics and Physical Sciences.* Trans. A.I. Dale. New York: Springer, 1998.
Lucretius. *On the Nature of Things.* Trans. Copley. New York: Norton, 1997.
Plato. *Parmenides.* Trans. Mary Louise Gill and Paul Ryan. Indianapolis: Hackett, 1996.
Newton, Isaac. *Principia.* Trans. Andrew Mott. Ed. Florian Cajori. U of California P, 1962.

Figures

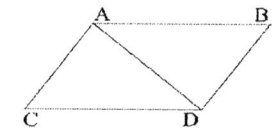

Figure 1: Diagram associated with Corollary I of the *Principia*

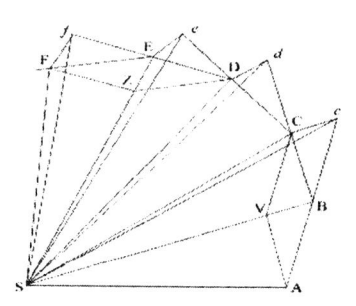

Figure 2 (above): Diagram from Section II, Proposition I, showing the way velocities increment in centripetal acceleration to produce an orbit (in the limit).

Euclid as Propadeutic

Patricia Cook
St. John's College, Annapolis

> Mathematics, making use of hypotheses, falls short of being the non-hypothetical and perfect science.... [Since] it is necessary to refer the benefit arising from [mathematics] to something else, we must connect that benefit with intellectual knowledge (*no-eran gnosin*) to which it leads the way and is propadeutic, clearing the eye of the soul and taking away the impediments which the senses place in the way of knowledge and universals ...
> —Proclus, *Commentary on Euclid* 1, 7-28.

Geometry is one of the seven traditional liberal arts, a member of the quadrivium of geometry, arithmetic, music, and astronomy. Accordingly, we study Euclid's geometry as we do any liberal arts text: for its own sake. There is an ancient anecdote that someone who had begun to study geometry with Euclid asked after he had learned the first theorem, "But what shall I get by learning these things?" Euclid called his slave and said, "Give him an *obol* [a coin], since he must gain from what he learns." Cicero says in the *Tusculan Disputations* that nothing was more brilliant in Greece than its mathematicians, and then he goes on to complain that the Romans limited its scope by studying it only for its utility for measurement and calculations (*Tusculan Disputations* 1.5). And of course geometry (literally, "earth measurement") indeed has an enormous range of practical applications. But let us not forget its intrinsic value, especially in light of what Proclus says (above) and what I am about to say. I am going to argue that Euclid is itself also propadeutic to much of what we call liberal education.

Study of Euclid is certainly propadeutic to the study of natural science. (To put this in terms of what Jim Beall was showing us in this morning's plenary address, geometry prepares us for study of "the liberal art of natural philosophy.") Apollonius, Archimedes, Ptolemy, Galileo, Kepler, and Newton all make use, with or without acknowledgment, of specific Euclidean proofs or theorems that were probably discovered by Euclid. Some natural philosophers use geometry only as a tool for scientific accounts. Others take mathematics to be the very language of nature. Those of us who were part of the NEH Seminar on "Bridging the Gap" between humanities and sciences were reminded last summer of some striking examples. Ptolemy claims "the earth has to the senses the ratio of a point to a distance of the sphere of the so-called fixed stars" (*The Almagest*, book I.6). Making the earth a point frees us to use the idealizations of geometry: Ptolemy later uses a pure Euclidean demonstration of the equivalence of the eccentric and epicycle-deferent systems. Galileo and Kepler make Euclidean geometry applicable to actual natural events (such as heavy falling bodies). Newton argues that Euclidean geometry is somehow coextensive with the science of mechanics, and he uses it to create a vision of the material universe from which we can calculate the minutest detail of a particular occurrence. These very uses of geometry raise one of the deepest questions about the rent between the sciences and the humanities. Is the metaphysic of mathematics the key to the natural world? Or is geometry only an extreme abstraction from the physical behavior of bodies? Does geometry involve turning away from the physical world in contemplation of the ideal, or does a mathematical account help us to understand something about the world ?

These considerations lead us to another way that Euclid is, or ought to be, propadeutic. Any form of teaching or learning makes presuppositions about the capacity of the human soul. Are there transcendent, universal truths that learners can come to recognize? Or is the learner in fact a blank slate, a mere receptor for transmission of the archives of what humans suppose is knowledge? Is there a priori knowledge? Is there synthetic a priori knowledge? Anyone who takes up Euclid's *Elements* has these questions laid before him. Most students working with Euclid come to believe what Augustine gives voice to in *The Confessions*, that "geometrical principles are neither Greek nor Latin nor any other kind of language

.... Lines, figures, numbers are not present to our minds as images, but as the mathematicals themselves." Indeed, "a person . . . knows them within himself" (*Confessions* book X, chapter xii). Is this true? If so, how are we to understand the human soul that has this power? What are the conditions for its possibility?

This brings us to what is perhaps the most significant respect in which Euclid is propadeutic. Euclid's *Elements* lays bare the very structure of human understanding. This great book, now more than twenty-two centuries old, presents plane geometry (books I-VI), arithmetic, theory of numbers (VII-X), and solid geometry (XI-XIII), by what we have come to call the axiomatic method. This seems to me to mirror the structure of discursive understanding of any topic whatsoever. Certain notions are taken as primitive, and all further notions are defined in terms of the primitive ones. Each geometrical term used by Euclid he defines; each of his thirteen books begins with a set of definitions. The first book opens with twenty-three definitions, and ten assumptions—which in most surviving manuscripts are grouped into five postulates and five axioms or common notions—and ends with the Pythagorean theorem and its converse. The series of thirteen books culminates with the construction of the five regular solids—the pyramid, cube, octahedron, icosahedron, and dodecahedron—compared as planar approximations of a sphere. But in studying Euclid, the student begins right where Euclid begins: with first things.

When we read Euclid at St. John's, we spend weeks talking about just the preliminaries. About his twenty-three Definitions, such as, "a point is that which has no part" or "a line is a breadthless length," we would ask: What makes for a good definition? Are Euclid's definitions arbitrary? What is Euclid's definition of a definition? Are any existential claims being made in the definitions? Are they empirical? Do the definitions eliminate physicality?

Of a Postulate such as #1, "let it be postulated to draw a straight line from any point to any point" or Postulate #5, the famous parallel postulate, "if a straight line falling on two straight lines makes the interior angles on the same side less than two right angles, then the two lines, if produced indefinitely, meet on that side on which are the angles less than two right angles," we would discuss whether this has the status of a hypothesis, whether it is provable, if it tied to human experience, whether it really ought to be a definition, and so on.

Similarly with the Common Notions, such as Common Notion #5, "the whole is greater than the part" or Common Notion #1, "things which are equal to the same thing are also equal to one another." Of course we would wonder about the difference between common notions and postulates. If the difference between the postulates and common notions seems to be, for example, that the postulates deal specifically with geometry while common notions are more general axioms about magnitude and are present in every subject, one should ask, is this self-evident? Does all human thought presuppose this? Does Euclid provide an adequate characterization of equality?

One would proceed to inquire about deductions and proofs. Is only logic involved? Do we have to use arithmetic in these inferences? What is the function of the diagrams Euclid provides? How complete is Euclid's system, that is, does he in fact assert all of the statements that it is in principle possible to derive? And so on. The study of Euclid, in short, offers a kind of pure opportunity to reflect on argument, upon the first principles upon which an argument depends, and on the role a deductive system can have in the crude flux of human experience.

Thinking about Euclid amounts to thinking about thought.

In the time that is left I want to make a final claim on behalf of Euclid as propadeutic, as preparation for further study, because it provides a pedagogical bridge between the humanities and sciences. Working with Euclid's *Elements* invites us to teach and to learn in the demonstrative mode. At St. John's we require that students learn theorems, memorize the proofs, and demonstrate them to fellow students. Participants did a bit of this at the "Bridging the Gap" Institute last summer. This seems at first to be a rote exercise, but in fact, it is quite significant: it underwrites the whole project of liberal education. In Euclid, students are liberated from dogma, from authoritative opinions, and are confronted with arguments to examine for themselves. Euclid never simply solicits acceptance of his propositions: he provides a precise chain of reasoning. His presuppositions are explicit, and are exposed to inquiry. The demonstrations demand nothing but careful attention and independent reason. Performing one of Euclid's demonstrations involves following—and understanding—every step. It cultivates the art of indicating assent or dissent in graduated terms. It acclimates one to the very small increments in which most learning occurs. Perhaps one can discover, from participating in this demonstrative mode, what it means to really understand.

Everyone has heard of the inscription over the porch of Plato's Academy that read, "Let no one un-versed in geometry enter my doors." Maybe Plato had all this in mind: that the study of geometry habituates students to see truth in light of evidence, and to take knowledge as their own possession.

Works Cited

Augustine. *Confessions*. Trans. Henry Chadwick. Oxford: Oxford UP, 2009.

Cicero. *Philosophical Treatises: Tusculan Disputations.* Vol. XVIII. Trans J.E. King. London: Loeb Classical Library, 1927.

Euclid. *Elements*. Trans. Thomas L. Heath. Ed. Dana Densmore. Santa Fe: Green Lion Press, 2002.

Proclus, Diadochus. *Commentary on the First Book of Euclid's* Elements. Princeton: Princeton UP, 1970.

Ptolemy. *Almagest.* Trans. G.J. Toomer. Princeton: Princeton UP, 1998.

Stealing the Power and Bridging the Gap: Ellison's *Invisible Man* as Core Text

Page Laws
Norfolk State University

> For now I had begun to believe, despite all the talk of science around me, that there was a magic in spoken words.
>
> So I denounce and I defend and I hate and I love.
> —Ralph Ellison, *Invisible Man*

Ellison's own technological bent apparently manifested itself in childhood as a passion for building radios (with a white friend named Hoolie, mentioned in *Shadow and Act*). As an adult Ellison earned supplemental income both as a photographer and as a "high-fidelity sound system installer," jobs he mentions in his introduction (vi-viii) to the 1981 edition of *Invisible Man*. All three pursuits are, of course, dead giveaways for a "techie" streak within Ellison's humanistic soul. What particularly interests me as a participant in the ongoing ACTC "Bridging the Gap Between the Humanities and Sciences" project, is not so much Ellison's own psychobiography as his radically ambivalent and wonderfully ironic depiction of science/technology versus the humanities in his virtuoso core text *Invisible Man*. The novel's core status just may rest, in fact, on the complex dialectics it embraces: science versus humanities, white power versus black spirituality. The rope (or trope) bridge Ellison throws across dialectical divides is metaphor: weak words twisted together into surprisingly strong strands of meaning. These bridges can and do, however, come unraveled—deconstruct—sometimes when one is standing on them.

One of the most memorable images in *Invisible Man* is that of the I-narrator holed up in an underground room he has brilliantly lit by stealing power from his city's electrical grid, the white-controlled Monopolated Light and Power. He has installed exactly 1,369 light bulbs—note the fetish for numbers—on the four walls, and plans to "start on the floor" (7)—only half aware, it seems, that this will give him no place to stand (cf. Archimedes' 'Give me a place to stand and I'll move the world"). Rendered invisible by racism and rendered a misfit by his odd, interrupted education at a fictitious black college, Ellison's clever narrator has a Promethean urge to seize both literal and figurative illumination from his oppressors. In his legitimate, humanistic desire to be "seen," he almost overcomes the gap between his limited knowledge and the supposed scientific superiority of his tormentors—almost. But that's getting too far ahead. As Ellison's I-narrator says to end his famous prologue, "Bear with me."

Before discussing electrification as one of Ellison's privileged metaphors, it may help to recall how frequent and felicitous is his use of *other* metaphors—including invisibility and blindness—throughout the novel. As memorable as the light bulb-studded underground room from which the I-narrator tells the whole novel in flashback is his first full anecdote from adolescence—the story of the Battle Royal. The leading white men in the I-narrator's town bring in a crowd of black high school boys, have them don boxing trunks and gloves, and then have them pummel each other bloody—all the while blindfolded. The young I-narrator, eager for a chance to deliver a Booker T. Washington-inspired speech, lets himself be thus manipulated and humiliated. The prize for his aggression against his fellow students—and his submissiveness to the whites—is a briefcase (a piece of emotional baggage he will drag around with him for the rest of the novel) and a scholarship to a black college which turns out to be run in neo-colonial fashion by a black administrator who lives only to kiss up to white millionaires. No better allegory for black-on-black violence exists in all of literature than Ellison's Battle Royal. Likewise, no better allegory for the hopes and let-downs of black higher education exists than Ellison's account of the I-narrator's college experience, cut short when he inadvertently crosses the college president. This vindictive president, Dr. Bledsoe (a BTW clone), packs our narrator off to New York—"out of the fire and into the melting pot" (150) bearing not-to-be-opened letters of 'recommendation' which turn out, instead, to be cruel dis-commendations. Ellison once more shows blacks displacing their anger at whites by violating one another, crabs-in-a-barrel style.

The only job the I-narrator can find in New York is working for a paint company—Liberty Paints—which manufactures a product called Optic White. The secret to the dazzling whiteness of this paint turns out to be drops of black paint—or should we blow the allegory and say blood?—meticulously mixed in. The man responsible for the paint's durable formula is not one of the highly paid white chemists, but the black man who works in the factory basement—Lucius Brockway. "We the machines inside the machine," says Brockway to the narrator (212). The I-narrator nearly blows up the place and is sent to recover at the factory hospital where he's wired up to a lobotomy machine. He eventually escapes and stumbles into a job with a communist group known only as the Brotherhood—thoroughly wedded to the scientific dictates of Marxist theory. The I-narrator eventually rebels at their manipulation and hypocrisy. He tangles with an emotional, infantile black nationalist—Ras the Exhorter. He's later mistaken for another metaphorical alter ego: the pimp/thug/preacher Rinehart whose heart is anything but pure (cf. the word "*rein*" in German). The I-narrator at one point hides out in a coal bin, quite aware of the insane aptness of his metaphorical situation—a black man seeking out the camouflage of coal and forced to light his way out of the darkness by burning the symbol of his education, an otherwise useless high school diploma.

Ellison's use of metaphor is so apt, so ingenious, that his verbal dexterity—his linguistic virtuosity—strikes a blow for justice far more powerful than any direct exhortation.

Let's return briefly to the metaphorical use of electricity and electrification throughout the novel. Douglas Ford in his article "Crossroads and Cross-Currents in Invisible Man," points out how often electricity enters the plot. At the Battle Royal, money is thrown on an electrified rug for the unwitting young black boxers to fight over. There is mention of electric clocks, electric loudspeakers, and an electric guitar. There is a power station built at the black college. The poor black 'peasant' Jim Trueblood lives so close to campus he can hear the station pounding away, but he gets no benefit from it. The bone-chilling cold in his cabin leads him to sleep in the same bed with both his wife and daughter, both of whom he impregnates. The 'lobotomy' machine at the hospital is, of course, a piece of electrical equipment, as is the I-narrator's radio-phonograph (Ford 889).

The I-narrator eventually masters the electrical grid or "network" more successfully than he is able to master either the 'old boy' network at his black college or the other social networks in New York. Says Ford, "Ultimately, no network remains impenetrable, the novel suggests—even those networks designed to maintain the invisibility of an entire population" (901). The dicey thing about technology is the way it can spread to its initial victims, giving them a weapon to turn back upon their oppressors. Ford notes how electrification brought in streetcars that eventually increased social mobility for blacks. Ford continues, ". . . The subversive appropriation of technology—or more specifically electricity—signifies an act of sabotage upon social norms and conventions" (888). In contemporary terms, one might think of the "digital divide" that still separates blacks and whites owning computers. On the other hand, consider the appropriation of the Internet by political extremists from underdeveloped countries.

John S. Wright has also written about Ellison's use of electrification as a major theme in his work. He calls Ellison's illuminated underground room a "riff" on Hemingway's 'A Clean, Well-Lighted Place" and Fitzgerald's *The Great Gatsby*—especially Daisy's green lit pier (191). Ellison indeed 'riffs' on other authors, from Dante to Melville to T. S. Eliot. Literary allusions—to dead, white canonical authors—can also be considered an act of appropriation.

A look at the diction of the prologue to *Invisible Man* shows Ellison chattily alluding to literature (H.G. Wells and Edgar Allan Poe), cinema, and the pseudo-science of spiritualism—all in the first two lines:

> I am an invisible man. No, I am not a spook like those who haunted Edgar Allan Poe; nor am I one of your Hollywood-movie ectoplasms. I am a man of substance, of flesh and bone, fiber and liquids—and I might even be said to possess a mind.

"Spook" is, of course, a pun worthy of Hamlet at his most cynical. It means ghost, but also is a racist epithet for a black person. The tone of the two lines mocks the baleful pseudo-science that underpins much of racist thought. One thinks, for instance, of phrenology—skull measurements performed on blacks well into the twentieth century in an effort to scientifically 'prove' their inferiority. "Flesh and bone" sounds both medical and faintly Biblical; "fiber and liquids" certainly sounds scientific: Metamucil comes to mind. The line ". . . Nor is my invisibility exactly a matter of a biochemical accident to my epidermis" is a complete parody of scientific jargon. Can the hot sun of equatorial Africa be considered a "biochemical accident" that produced increased amounts of melanin in the "epidermis" of Africans? The I-narrator continues, "That invisibility to which I refer occurs because of a peculiar disposition of the eyes of those with whom I come in contact" (3). Note the careful and formal wording to avoid dangling prepositions: "to which" instead of the more colloquial 'which I refer to'; "with whom" instead of 'who I come in contact with'. The phrase "peculiar disposition" sounds suspiciously like "peculiar institution" (i.e. slavery). The general tone resembles is that of an epidemiologist discussing the spread of a disease, in this case the dread 'disease' of being black.

The I-narrator moves on to discuss the white man who ran into him and whom he felt obliged to beat up. Here the tone becomes almost psychiatric. The white man was "in the midst of a walking nightmare," and the I-narrator clearly sees, in retrospect, that he, a black man walking along the street, represented the white man's repression incarnate: "Something in this man's thick head had sprung out and beaten him within an inch of his life" (4-5). Psychiatrist, anthropologist, political scientist—in the remainder of the prologue Ellison skillfully apes them all. Who but an anthropologist speaks of the "important distinction" between the terms "civilization" and "culture" (cf. 6). Who but an anthropologist would think of the aboriginal boomerang as a continuing metaphor—almost a conceit—for the cyclical nature of Ellisonian thought.

Both scientist and philosopher, Ellison rises above disciplinary distinctions. Alluding one moment to Dante and the next to African American slave history, Ellison is both preacher-teacher and "thinker-tinker." The I-narrator compares himself to the great American technologists such as Ford, Edison, and Franklin. But he's equally a Hamlet, or, later in the novel, a Southern-fried Sartre: "I yam what I am" (260).

Ellison seems very skeptical about Marxist "science" and discipline, but he doesn't abandon the humanistic impulse behind

Marxism. And he remains very much the dialectician—keeping opposites in tension/balance and encompassing both electrical poles: positive and negative. A number of critics have noted the use of musical virtuosity—jazz riffing—as the black artist's means to mastery. Ellison helps us see that musical notes, scientific numbers, *and* words—all can and must be mastered before the oppressed can rise to the level of their techno-savvy oppressors.

Works Cited

Ellison, Ralph. *Invisible Man*. New York: Vintage Books, 1972.

Ford, Douglas. "Crossroads and Cross-Currents in Invisible Man." *Modern Fiction Studies* 45.4 (1999): 887-904.

Wright, John S. "'Jack-the-Bear' Dreaming: Ellison's Spiritual Technologies." *boundary* 2 30.2 (2003): 175-194.

Connecting Principles in Adam Smith's *History of Astronomy*

Charles Sullivan
University of Dallas

In May 1766, the French actress and popular novelist Madame Ricoboni met Adam Smith in Paris. "My God, what a Scot!" she declared, "He speaks harshly, with big teeth, and he's ugly as the devil. He's Mr. Smith, author of a book I haven't read." Soon, however, she was singing a very different tune. "He's a most absent-minded creature, but one of the most good-hearted." And in October, after Smith had returned to Britain, she lamented his departure. "I like Mr. Smith. I like him greatly. I wish that the devil would carry off all of our *gens de lettres*, all of our *philosophes*, and bring Mr. Smith back to me. Superior people seek him out" (Nicholls, 71). Smith's fortunes in the liberal arts core curriculum have not been unlike his shifting fortunes in Madame Riccoboni's esteem. Smith's *Wealth of Nations*, perhaps the canonical text in political economy in English-speaking universities throughout the world, is too long and often too technical—in a word, too awkward—for anything but the most abridged selections. And, for many, what are presumed to be its *laissez-faire* principles speak too harshly.

Long eclipsed by the preeminence of the *Wealth of Nations*, Smith's *Theory of Moral Sentiments* has, within the last generation of scholarship, found its way into the canon of ethics—I think here, in particular, of Charles Griswold's *Adam Smith and the Virtues of Enlightenment*. Recent attention to the *Theory of Moral Sentiments* has, in turn, led to a rethinking of the place of the *Wealth of Nations* in the canon. We are now more likely, for example, to detect the ethical-economic overlay in the capital accumulation argument of book II. We are more likely to read book V on the education of youth. And we are more likely to understand Smith's entire project in terms of a commercial humanism's language of manners. In sum, we, like Madame Riccoboni in 1766, discover a more "goodhearted" Smith. Still, for all the richness of recent Smith scholarship, relatively little attention has been directed to such works as Smith's lectures on rhetoric and *belles-lettres* or Smith's so-called essays on philosophical subjects that were posthumously published in 1790.

I want to look at one of those philosophical essays—the "History of Astronomy."[1] Internal evidence indicates that Smith drafted the essay sometime before 1758, perhaps during his years as a student at Oxford University when he was reading (in addition to David Hume's *Treatise on Human Nature*) the works of the French *philosophes* Condillac, D'Alembert, and Diderot. Smith's literary executors, the chemist Joseph Black and the geologist James Hutton, explained in their introduction to the essay that Smith had originally intended it to be part of "a connected history of the liberal sciences and elegant arts." Smith, they continued, "had found it necessary to abandon that plan as far too extensive." Nonetheless, when Smith, shortly before his death, ordered the destruction of sixteen volumes of unpublished writings, he spared what remained of this projected history (31). Alongside the "History of Astronomy," we have a "History of Ancient Physics," a "History of Ancient Logic and Metaphysics," an essay on the "External Senses," and two essays on the "Imitative Arts." Among these writings, the "History of Astronomy" played a critical role. It was here that Smith proposed to harmonize the spheres and lay out the general "principles that lead and direct philosophical enquiry."

Smith grounded his history of astronomy, and hence his understanding of "the principles that lead and direct philosophical enquiry," in a progress of three sentiments. The sentiment that Smith called "Surprise" arose from the experience of the unexpected: a violent and sudden change in our situation occasions a violent and convulsive movement in our emotions. What is new and singular gives rise to the sentiment of "Wonder." Wonder occurs when we have a strange experience that "refuses to be grouped" with the other classes of phenomena with which we are familiar or when an appearance not out of the ordinary in itself refuses to "fall in with" the association of ideas to which we are accustomed. Memory and imagination "hesitate," "uneasy" and "anxious," "uncertain" what to think and "undetermined" what to do. "The stop which is thereby given to the career of the imagination," Smith wrote, "the difficulty which it finds in passing along such disjointed objects, and the feeling of something like a gap or interval betwixt them, constitute the whole essence of this emotion" (42). Smith also identified a third sentiment. The experience of the great or the beautiful excited what he called "Admiration."

In "the first ages of society," Smith continued, the sentiment of Surprise predominates. Where "subsistence is precarious" and where the savage, "unprotected by the laws," is daily exposed to every danger, mankind's passions alternate between "terror and consternation" on the one hand and "reverence and gratitude" on the other hand. And as we, according to Smith, tend to explain things to ourselves by analogy to those phenomena with which we are most familiar, the savage models polytheism on his own vigorous, but thwarted, will. What Emile Durkheim would later call the *conscience collective*—the collective consciousness—conceives every object of an unmastered nature as the manifestation of the anger or the favor of capricious gods (48-50). With the rise of civilization—a development that Smith assigns to the ancient Greeks—the sentiment of Surprise yields to the sentiment of Wonder. As law establishes greater security, the fears of mankind diminish; as subsistence becomes less precarious, the magnanimity and cheerfulness of society grow apace. "Men of liberal fortune" now have the leisure to contemplate "the great objects of nature" and they seek "to render the whole course of the universe consistent and of a piece." Thus philosophy has its origins for Adam Smith not in our needs and interests but in the absence of need and interest. Wonder, Smith concludes, "not the expectation of advantage" from discovery "prompts" mankind to "study of philosophy" and "the connecting principles of nature" (50-51).

Greatest among the objects of nature are the phenomena of astronomy. According to Smith's history, philosophers such as Aristotle first brought coherence to these phenomena in a "System of Concentric Spheres" in which the Fixed Stars, the Sun, and the Moon revolved in constant velocities around the earth. The discovery of Wandering Stars, or Planets, necessitated the introduction of ever more spheres, while the appearance of retrograde motions perplexed the imagination. Ptolemy's System of Epicycles momentarily relieved the embarrassment, but new discoveries—what T.S. Kuhn in the *Structure of Scientific Revolutions* called "anomalies"—required the addition of more and more complex epicycles. Hence, too, the System of Epicycles became in turn "too intricate and complex" for "the imagination to rest in it with complete tranquility and satisfaction." For, Smith explained, "systems" are like "imaginary machines," and it is not enough that they merely work. They may be improved to do the same work with fewer motions (66-67).

Enter a workshop, Smith urged, in all likelihood thinking of the *encyclopédistes* d'Alembert and Diderot. For the "common artizan" the familiar operations of his particular art excite little curiosity. Yet, to the "practiced thought of a philosopher," custom had obscured the connecting principles. Much as in music, there may be an agreeable harmony and measure to the "careless" listener where to the "practiced ear" the most exact time, the most perfect coincidence, is missing. Implicit in this double metaphor is a critical shift in the role of philosophy. Where philosophy had initially served to calm the Surprise and Wonder of an anxious imagination, it now served to call an "indolent imagination" (86) to the sentiment of Admiration for the great and beautiful. Thus the subsequent history of astronomy now upset common expectations and comfortable habits of thought: the heliocentric System of Copernicus and Galileo challenged a traditional anthropocentrism; Kepler's laws of planetary motion challenged a belief in the perfection of circular motion; Descartes' System of Vortices challenged an idea of natural inertia; and, most importantly, Newton's law of gravitational attraction challenged a familiar mechanics of impulse.

For readers of core texts and for instructors in core curricula, the account that Smith offers of "the natural career of the imagination" in the "History of Astronomy" is significant, I think, for at least three reasons. Consider, first, the common view that Smith's *Wealth of Nations* merits a place in the western canon because it is the starting point for a "science" of economics. On an initial reading, the argument of the "History of Astronomy" may seem to converge with a sociological positivism. Indeed the nineteenth-century French philosopher Auguste Comte read the essay in just this way, assimilating its principles to his own law of the three states and hierarchy of the six sciences. But, on closer examination, we see that Smith himself was arguing that "all philosophical systems"—even Newton's law of gravitation—were "mere inventions of the imagination" (105), justified to be sure by their ability to provide coherent accounts of phenomena, but justified also by aesthetic criteria of simplicity and beauty. Thus, the "History of Astronomy," in the manner that it foregrounds the role of the imagination and, in effect, humanizes the sciences, warns us conversely of scientizing the humanities.

Consider, second, how the "History of Astronomy" fits into the relationship between the *Theory of Moral Sentiments* and the *Wealth of Nations*—a relationship that increasingly defines Smith's place in the western canon. In the 1759 edition of the *Theory of Moral Sentiments*, Smith, like Hume, used sympathy and the impartial spectator as connecting principles. But, unlike Hume, Smith understood these principles not in terms of an "interested obligation" but in terms of "self-command." In 1776, in the *Wealth of Nations*, Smith complemented his account of sympathy, a principle that, as he conceded, weakened the greater the social distance, with an account of the division of labor, a principle that grew stronger the greater the extent of the market. Yet Smith also warned that the productivity and interdependence occasioned by the division of labor had a moral cost. "The man whose whole life is spent in performing a few simple operations," Smith wrote in Book V on the Education of Youth, "has no occasion to exert his understanding, or to exercise his invention.... The torpor of his mind renders him, not only incapable of relishing or bearing a part in any rational conversation, but conceiving any generous, noble, or tender sentiment" (302-3). In the *Wealth of Nations*, Smith had placed his hope in "those few, who, being attached to no particular occupation themselves," acquire a "comprehensive" understanding of society. Likewise in the 1790 edition of the *Theory of Moral Sentiments*, Smith contrasted the "inferior prudence" of the frugal man, who was content with mere "propriety," to the "superior prudence" of "the wise and virtuous man" who "endeavours as well as he can to assimilate his own character to [the] archetype of perfection" (292).

To be sure, when "History of Astronomy" made the task of philosophy to "get rid of Wonder," Smith lent his voice to what Max Weber called the "disenchantment of the world." But he did so only to free the imagination from the anxiety that accompanied a worldview built around the accidental and the arbitrary. He did not do so to turn the imagination over to "the workshop" of "the common artisan" or to an "iron cage" of the invisible hand. Indeed, Smith first used the phrase "invisible hand" in the "History of Astronomy" to refer to the pusillanimous superstitions of primitive polytheism. Thus, the "History of Astronomy," in the way that it links the "principles that lead and direct philosophical enquiry" to Wonder, warns us not to fetishize the market and immediate advantage.[2] As Spencer Pack has observed, the notion of an "invisible hand" refers not to a divine providence or to a natural necessity, but rather to a convenient fiction or metaphor. "Whether it is best to leave the economy alone, to the workings of a perceived invisible hand, is for Smith an empirical question, not a religious or metaphysical one" (293).

Finally, consider how Smith's "History of Astronomy" speaks to the role of a liberal educator. We have just seen that one purpose of a liberal education is to free the imagination—to emancipate it from contingency into a civilized world ruled by law and public reason. Yet at another level, the natural career of the imagination did not end with what we might call "the push" of Surprise. In fact, it was precisely here that Smith turned philosophy against an indolent imagination. Earlier, I invoked Durkheim's notion of *conscience collective* to capture something of the link that Smith establishes between social evolution and cultural outlook. But note that the French contains a productive ambiguity. It may also be rendered the collective conscience. Smith's conception of philosophy, I am arguing, contains a similar productive ambiguity.[3] Recall that, beginning with Copernicus, the philosopher had upset anthropocentrism, circular motion, natural inertia, and the familiar (and we might add "political") mechanics of impulse. By Smith's own principle of analogy, we can also say that the function of a liberal education is to upset narcissism, parochialism, social inertia, and coercion and to redirect and elevate the imagination toward objects that, as Smith cites Aristotle, are "good for their own sake." In the end, Smith's "History of Astronomy" does not so much "get rid of Wonder" as open it to what we might call "the pull" of the Sentiment of Admiration for the Great and Beautiful.[4] And the "philosopher" does not merely soothe the collective consciousness of society, she also safeguards its collective conscience. Once again, with Madame Riccoboni, we move from first impressions of external refinements to a deeper appreciation of moral culture.

Notes

1. The version of the "History of Astronomy" that I am using may be found in Adam Smith, *Essays on Philosophical Subjects.*
2. Cf. Edmund Burke, *Reflections on the Revolution in France*: "Commerce and trade and manufacture" are "the gods of our economical politicians . . . which, as first causes, we choose to worship" (69).
3. As I understand it, Smith's argument in the "History of Astronomy" resembles Kant's argument in the essay "Idea for a Universal History from a Cosmopolitan Point of View." In that essay, Kant wrote that "nature is utterly unconcerned that man live well, only that he bring himself to the point where his conduct makes him worthy of life and well-being." That point, however, is not the terminus of human possibility. Again Kant observes, this time implicitly criticizing Hume and the French apologists for sociability, "We are, to high degree, cultivated beyond bearing by all manner of social convention and propriety. But we are a long way from being able to regard ourselves as moral. For the idea of morality belongs to culture, and yet using this idea only in reference to semblances of morality ... constitutes mere civilization." Indeed Kant worries that mere civilization may succumb to "soulless opulence." How, according to Kant, do we move from an enlightened age to an age of enlightenment, how do we avoid the danger of soulless opulence and attain moral culture. "The Idea," Kant writes, "may help, though only from afar." Philosophical education, in other words, may provide a "guiding thread," a form of cultural government that both respects the autonomy so critical to Kant's conception of ethics and redirects the imagination to its proper objects.
4. For the distinction between "push" and "pull," see Albert O. Hirschman, *Shifting Involvements: Private Interest and Public Action*, 5.

Works Cited

Burke, Edmund. *Reflections on the Revolution in France*. Indianapolis: Hackett, 1987.

Hirschman, Albert O. *Shifting Involvements: Private Interest and Public Action*. Princeton: Princeton UP, 1982.

Kant, Emmanuel. "Idea for a Universal History from a Cosmopolitan Point of View." Yale Press.
<http://yalepress.yale.edu/yupbooks/excerpts/kant_perpetual.pdf>.
Nicholls, James C., ed., "Mme Riccoboni's Letters to David Hume, David Garrick, and Sir Robert Liston, 1764-1783." *Studies on Voltaire and the Eighteenth Century* 149 (1976). 471p.
Pack, Spencer J. "Theological (and Hence Economic) Implications of Adam Smith's 'Principles which Lead and Direct Philosophical Enquiries." *History of Political Economy* 27.2 (1995).
Smith, Adam. *Essays on Philosophical Subjects.* Indianapolis: Liberty Classics, 1982.
---. "History of Astronomy." *Essays on Philosophical Subjects.* Indianapolis: Liberty Classics, 1982. 31-105.
---. *The Theory of Moral Sentiments.* Ed. Knud Haakonssen. Cambridge: Cambridge UP, 2002.
---. *Wealth of Nations.* New York: Penguin Classics, 1982.

Darwin Redux: Great Texts and Natural Sciences Revisited

Keith Francis
Baylor University

> The words of the wise are like goads, their collected sayings like firmly embedded nails—given by one Shepherd. Be warned, my son, of anything in addition to them. Of making many books there is no end, and much study wearies the body.
> —Ecclesiastes 12:12

> We don't need no education
> We don't need no thought control
> No dark sarcasm in the classroom
> Teachers leave the kids alone
> Hey teacher leave us kids alone
> All in all it's just another brick in the wall
> All in all you're just another brick in the wall
> —Pink Floyd "Another Brick in the Wall, Part II"

Although it seems somewhat incongruous to begin a paper dealing with liberal education with two statements which are, ostensibly, anti-education, it seems to me that the quotations represent one attitude towards the idea of using science in core texts, great texts, and honors programs. The attitude is rarely expressed explicitly, and it is usually kept in check by being hidden under a veneer of a liberal, meaning 'tolerant,' acceptance of all the disciplines in the liberal arts. Given the title of this paper, it will come as no surprise that I am referring to belief that science is a step-sister or subordinate discipline compared to disciplines such as literature or philosophy in core texts, great texts, and honors programs. Students in these programs do plenty of reading, thinking, and writing: what they do not do, quite literally, is science.

I am not arguing that science is ignored. In fact, a person looking would not have to search very hard in order to find a core text program in which famous scientific works such as Bacon's *Novum Organum* or Darwin's *The Descent of Man* are read.[1] I might even go so far as to argue that the presence of ancient authors such as Euclid and Ptolemy in college curricula is largely a result of great books or great texts programs. The reading is not the problem—there may be too much reading, to paraphrase the author of the saying I quoted from Ecclesiastes: the problem is in the doing. Students in core texts programs may read Ptolemy but they rarely do Ptolemy's experiments as part of their program.

Why is the doing so important? Quite simply because doing is an essential component of modern science. The 'new man' whom Bacon writes about so eloquently in *Novum Organum* is a person who does not subscribe to the old ways of looking at the world. The new man has not rejected authority, but he does test it. The new woman, to use a phrase that might have surprised Bacon, observes, experiments, analyzes, writes, and then believes. If that is the case, it is appropriate to ask: do students in core texts programs do proper science?

Before answering this question, like every student will do on at least one occasion, I must make a couple of excuses. First, because the humanities emphasize reading and writing and the sciences do not—a statement which is patently untrue if one thinks about it for more than a minute but is a useful myth—it makes sense to organize courses around the humanities. It also makes sense to read about science rather than do science. Second—and, I admit, less of a myth—the great texts of science are not easily accessible for a non-specialist (never mind a student). A former colleague of mine who was a scientist and a great admirer of Newton described *The Mathematical Principles of Natural Philosophy*, the *Principia*, as the most boring and obtuse book he had ever read. He suggested that I not use *Principia* in an honors course as it might "turn students off science"!

Is it possible to cut these two Gordian knots? Obviously, given the title of my paper, I believe the answer to this question is "yes." More particularly, I would argue that Charles Darwin's scientific methodology provides a way to bridge the gap between the need to do science and the tendency to read about science.

No one will doubt that *The Origin of Species by Means of Natural Selection, or the Preservation of Favoured Races in the Struggle for Life* (1859), to give the book its full title, is a great work of science. Darwin's "imperfect abstract," as he called it, still provokes controversy (65). And yet, as more than one commentator has noted, the book is easy to read and understand. John W. Barrow, the author of the introduction to the Penguin edition of *The Origin of Species*, draws attention to the fact that the book "was meant to be, and was, read by the general educated public" (11). I would go farther; because Darwin avoids technical language and organizes his argument in a simple and logic fashion, *The Origin of Species* is an ideal work of science to use in a core text, great texts, or honors course.

While it is true that Darwin's argument is a lucid and persuasive one—Thomas Huxley famously commented, "How stupid not to have realized that before!" and in Darwin's words from his autobiography, "It has convinced not a few able men"—it is worth taking the time to notice the organization of *The Origin of Species* (140). It is the clear and logical organization of the book that helps to make it so accessible to the non-specialist. For example, at the beginning of each chapter, Darwin includes an outline of the main points of the chapter. If readers find themselves lost in botanical, zoological, or geological detail, they can return to the beginning of the chapter and find their place in the overall argument again. Or, for those with an affinity for Cliff Notes, it is possible to follow Darwin's whole argument throughout *The Origin of Species* by reading all the summaries at the beginning of each chapter in succession.

Furthermore, because Darwin wanted readers of *The Origin of Species* to follow his argument and not miss any of the points he made, at the conclusion of all the chapters except three, nine, and eleven there is a summary of the main points.[2] (Darwin clearly had the potential to become the kind of lecturer students prefer if they have to take notes.) Again, for those who have not read *The Origin of Species*, it is possible to follow and learn the whole of Darwin's argument just by reading the chapter summaries—a redundancy no sane publisher would allow these days!

Last with regard to organization, Darwin included a large number of practical examples in *The Origin of Species*. Of course, Darwin wanted to make his argument convincing to the specialists, and so he had to provide evidence for his assertions, but I also think that Darwin cared about his non-specialist readers' powers of concentration. At times in the book, it is almost as if Darwin is thinking, "Well, that last portion of the argument was a bit difficult to follow, let me illustrate it with an example." The reader's response is meant to be, "Ah, that's what he was trying to say!" For example, in the first chapter entitled 'Variation under Domestication,' having engaged in an extended argument about the difficulty of differentiating between varieties and species, Darwin gives a simple example of the problem—the reader is given the opportunity to take a metaphorical breath:

> I have discussed the probable origin of domestic pigeons at some . . . length; because when I first kept pigeons and watched the several kinds, knowing well how true they bred, I felt fully as much difficulty in believing that they could ever have descended from a common parent, as any naturalist could in coming to a similar conclusion in regard to the many species of finches, or other large groups of birds, in nature. One circumstance has struck me much; namely, that all the breeders of the various domestic animals and the cultivators of plants, with whom I have ever conversed, or whose treatises I have read, are firmly convinced that the several breeds to which each has attended, are descended from so many aboriginally distinct species. Ask, as I have asked, a celebrated raiser of Hereford cattle, whether his cattle might not have descended from long-horns, and he will laugh you to scorn. I have never met a pigeon, or poultry, or duck, or rabbit fancier, who was not fully convinced that each main breed was descended from a distinct species. (88)

Darwin's organization of *The Origin of Species*—the ease with which the reader is taken through what is a complicated and complex problem in science—set me thinking about Darwin's writing style and the way he did science. How did Darwin approach doing and recording science? Answering my own question, it seemed to me that Darwin was a keen observer of nature: he is rightly called a naturalist. Was this method, this observation and recording of nature in action, easily replicable? And, more important with regard to core texts courses, great texts courses, and honors programs, could this method be used to help students taking these courses do science rather than reading and discussing science? Certainly, any student using Darwin's method would be doing basic natural science: observing a particular phenomenon in nature over a period of time, recording the results, and considering the larger implications of those results. Again, given the title of the paper, it is probably clear that I believe Darwin's method can be replicated in the classroom of a core texts or great texts course.

In order to defend my assertion, I want to cheat a little. Rather than use *The Origin of Species*, which is an extended argument about evolution by natural selection, I would like to suggest some possibilities for the classroom by referring to a couple of Darwin's lesser-known and less-frequently-read works. In *The Origin of Species,* Darwin presents the results of his and others' experiments: there's little emphasis on doing the science and a major emphasis on the meaning of the science. However, in *The Expression of Emotions in Man and Animals*, published 1872, and *The Formation of Vegetable Mould, Through the Action of Worms, with Observations on Their Habits*, published 1881, the two books to which I will refer, Darwin describes the experiments at the foundation of some of his theories in much more detail.[3] In other words, Darwin permits the reader to 'see' him doing science as much as theorizing about implications of scientific observation. (And, following Darwin's usual practice, there are outlines at the beginning of each chapter in order to make his argument easy to follow.)

Although I am cheating by not using *The Origin of Species*, it is important to note that Darwin himself considered these later works explications of his theory of evolution. "We have seen that the study of the theory of expression confirms to a certain limited extent the conclusion that man is derived from some lower animal form, and supports the belief of the specific or sub-specific unity of several races," comments Darwin in the concluding chapter of *The Expression of Emotions in Man and Animals*, "but as far as my judgment serves, such confirmation was hardly needed" (367). By Darwin's usual cautious standards, the latter comment is a bold statement of his position; Darwin was reacting to leading anatomists such as Charles Bell (1774-1842) and Richard Owen (1804-1892), who argued that the human brain or certain groups of human muscles were specially created for the function they served, and thus humans were different, "higher," than animals such as monkeys or apes, a distinct and special creation made at a particular point in time by God.[4] For this paper, the point to note is that Darwin considered he was giving more evidence for his theory. Darwin never wrote the large book on evolution that he intended—he mentions in his autobiography that "had I published on the scale in which I began to write in 1856, the book would have been four or five times as large as the *Origin*," but the essay of Alfred Wallace (1823-1913) on natural selection which Darwin received in1858 pre-empted this—but his later works did explain some of the natural phenomena that could be observed and the scientific experiments that could be used to demonstrate the validity of his theory (124).

The genius of Darwin's method and a key reason why it can be used in the classroom is its simplicity. Complex experiments that might require thousands of pounds of laboratory equipment were not Darwin's forte. The ability to observe and the patience to record a large amount of data are the necessary requirements for professors and students who want to emulate Darwin. For example, in order to compile the data for *The Expression of Emotions in Man and Animals*—a book of 367 pages—Darwin says that he observed infants, studied the insane (who were "liable to the strongest passions"), observed an old man who had electrical currents applied to his facial muscles and studied the pictures of his reactions, looked at photographs and engravings of "great masters in painting and sculpture," circulated a questionnaire to missionaries and people outside of England (with questions such as "Is laughter ever carried to such an extreme as to bring tears into the eyes?"), and studied the expressions in some common animals like dogs and cats (13-17). Apart from the experiment on the old man—the "galvanizing" of anyone might not meet with the approval of a university committee on human experimentation—most of Darwin's experiments could be repeated with the appropriate preparation.[5]

In *The Formation of Vegetable Mould, Through the Action of Worms, with Observations on Their Habits,* Darwin makes life even easier for professors and students who want to do science. In this book Darwin includes the theses and the experiments that can be used to corroborate them side-by-side. The experiment, the result, and the larger theory that can be deduced from the result are all together; a humanities professor with little experience of conducting a science laboratory should be able to do Darwin's experiments. To illustrate, I will give three examples.

One basic component of contemporary scientific methodology is the devising of experiments to test general propositions. In these cases, the scientists want to create experiments that will confirm that they are heading in the right direction with regard to a particular theory, and, if possible, the experiment will suggest other avenues of investigation. In the introduction to *The Formation of Vegetable Mould, Through the*

Action of Worms, with Observations on Their Habits, Darwin describes a simple experiment done along this line:

> As I was led to keep in my study during many months worms in pots filled with earth, I became interested in them, and wished to learn how far they acted consciously, and how much mental power they displayed. I was the more desirous to learn something on this head, as few observations of this kind have been made, as far as I know, on animals so low in the scale of organization and so poorly provided with sense-organs, as are earth-worms. (2-3)

It certainly would not be difficult, or expensive, for the students in a core texts or great texts course to keep and observe worms in order to help them think about larger questions in the disciplines of anatomy, zoology, and even psychology.

A common type of experiment done by scientists is one in which they attempt to extend knowledge. A particular set of details is known about a phenomenon or an organism, and the question scientists ask is how much more can be known. Darwin provides a simple experiment that would enable students to engage in this methodology:

> Earth-worms must be considered as terrestrial animals, though they are still in one sense semi-aquatic, like the other members of the great class of annelids to which they belong. M. Perrier found that their exposure to the dry air of a room for only a single night was fatal to them. On the other hand he kept several large worms alive for nearly four months, completely submerged in water. (12-13)

Students could ask a number of questions that would extend their knowledge of earthworms. Example of these might be: Can every earthworm survive in water? Is the size of the earthworm related to its ability to survive in water? Do factors such as temperature and pressure affect the survival of earthworms in water? By asking questions such as these they could test Darwin's statement that earthworms "are still in one sense semi-aquatic."

Perhaps the best-known scientific endeavor is the experiment that enables scientists to confirm or reject a theory. To give this methodology a Darwinian twist, knowledge is extended by selecting those theories best suited to survive. In that vein, Darwin was able to reject one theory about earthworms by simple observation and measurement:

> It has often been said that under ordinary circumstances healthy worms never, or very rarely, completely leave their burrows at night; but this is an error, as White of Selborne long ago knew. In the morning, after there has been heavy rain, the film of mud or of very fine sand over gravel-walks is often plainly marked with their tracks. I have noticed this from August to May, both months included, and it probably occurs during the two remaining months of the year when they are wet. On these occasions, very few dead worms could anywhere be seen. On January 31, 1881, after a long-continued and unusually severe frost with much snow, as soon as a thaw set in, the walks were marked with innumerable tracks. On one occasion, five tracks were counted crossing a space of only an inch square. They could sometimes be traced either to or from the mouths of the burrow in the gravel-walks. (14-15)

Although this experiment might be more difficult to replicate, the important point to note is that the experiment itself was not difficult. Darwin simply observed the ground after it had rained for ten months. What the experiment did require, however, was some knowledge about the habits of earthworms. In this case, the professor leading the course would have to direct the students' reading before the students could conduct the experiment.

While leading or teaching core texts and great texts courses should never be described as easy, relying on the reading and discussing of these texts can lead to a kind of laziness. It becomes too easy to think of science as another set of ideas that students need to analyze. But philosophy and zoology cannot be treated exactly the same. In fact, the opposite needs to occur. In core texts and great texts courses students need to know that thinking by doing is just as important as thinking by reading, writing, or discussing. The ideas of science come into play as and while the experiments are being done. Theory and practice are intimately related.[6]

Darwin understood this. While it may require more preparation on the part of professors, students will begin to gain an appreciation of the larger questions of science when they become used to observing and acting the way scientists do. It is possible to teach this skill by beginning with simple experiments—perhaps what might be best described as the observation of everyday phenomena—and then 'graduating' to more complex ones.[7] Ultimately, it is the doing of science that makes science interesting. When discussing the relationship between his theory of evolution and "the theory of expression" Darwin—in *The Expression of the Emotions in Man and Animals*—argued that, "To understand, as far as possible, the source or origin of the various expressions which may be hourly seen on the faces of the men around us, not to mention our domesticated animals, ought to possess much interest for us" (367). Students can derive the same level of interest from investigating, "doing," any of the branches of science.

Notes

1. At the institution where I taught before coming to Baylor University, Pacific Union College in California, the Honors Program, a great texts program, uses these two works, the first in a seminar entitled Cosmos, the second in a seminar entitled Progress.
2. Chapters I, II, IX and XIV have a summary, but Darwin does not label these "Summary." In the case of the Chapter III, "Struggle for Existence," Darwin continues the argument in the next chapter in his discussion of natural selection, and so he summarizes both chapters. In Chapter IX, "On the Imperfection of the Geological Record," Darwin leaves the summary until the end of Chapter X, "On the Geological Succession of Organic Beings," labeling it "Summary of preceding and present chapters"; the same is true of Chapters XI and XII which are both about the geographical distribution of species. Chapter XIV is the last chapter of *The Origin of Species* in which Darwin recapitulates the argument in the whole book; the summary is a plea to scientists to take his theory seriously, really a peroration.
3. Although these books are not as well known as *The Origin of Species* or *The Descent of Man*, they are readily available in paperback.
4. Bell wrote *Essays on the Anatomy of Expression in Painting* that was first published in 1806; Darwin consulted the third edition that was published in 1844. Owen was one of the foremost scientists who opposed the idea of evolution; apart from his work on anatomy, he is best known for coining the word 'dinosaur' and being the designer and first director of The Natural History Museum in London.
5. Darwin has some fascinating, and also amusing, pictures and diagrams that illustrate his experiments. See *The Expression of Emotions in Man and Animals*, 52-55, 128, 141 and plates 1-7.
6. The same can be said for other disciplines such as music, the visual arts, and tactile arts.

7. Philip Sloan, President of the Association of Core Texts and Courses (ACTC) and Chair of the Liberal Studies Program at the University of Notre Dame, has devised some experiments with fruit flies—one of the commonly used species for experiments in genetics—that he is happy to share.

Works Cited

Barrow, John W. Introduction. *Origin of the Species*. By Charles Darwin. New York: Penguin, 1985.

Darwin, Charles. *The Autobiography of Charles Darwin 1809-1882*. Ed. Nora Barlow. London: Collins, 1958.

---. *The Expression of the Emotions in Man and Animals*. London: John Murray, 1904

---. *The Formation of Vegetable Mould, Through the Action of Worms, with Observations on Their Habits*. Whitefish, MT: Kessinger Publishing, 2004.

---. *The Origin of Species*. New York: Penguin, 1985.